I Heart Hedgehogs

This book is dedicated
to all hedgehogs that are,
that have been and that
are yet to come.
May you continue to
grace our gardens and
countryside with your
snuffling presence.

I Heart Hedgehogs

How to care for our lovable prickly friends

Pesala Bandara

HarperCollins*Publishers*
1 London Bridge Street
London SE1 9GF

www.harpercollins.co.uk

HarperCollins*Publishers*
Macken House, 39/40 Mayor Street Upper
Dublin 1, D01 C9W8, Ireland

First published by HarperCollins*Publishers* 2026
1 3 5 7 9 10 8 6 4 2

Text © Pesala Bandara
Flower and leaf illustrations: Shutterstock.com.
All other illustrations © Ollie Mann

Pesala Bandara asserts the moral right to be identified as the author of this work

A catalogue record of this book is available from the British Library

ISBN 978-0-0-881706-0

Printed and bound in the UK using 100% renewable electricity at
CPI Group (UK) Ltd

All rights reserved. No part of this publication may be reproduced, stored in
a retrieval system, or transmitted, in any form or by any means, electronic,
mechanical, photocopying, recording or otherwise, without the prior written
permission of the publishers.

Without limiting the exclusive rights of any author, contributor or the publisher
of this publication, any unauthorised use of this publication to train generative
artificial intelligence (AI) technologies is expressly prohibited. HarperCollins
also exercise their rights under Article 4(3) of the Digital Single Market Directive
2019/790 and expressly reserve this publication from the text and data mining
exception.

CONTENTS

Introduction –
Why We Love Hedgehogs.............................6

Get to Know Your Hedgehog 10

The Secret Life of Hedgehogs 26

Hogs in History and Folklore......................60

Be More Hedgehog......................................116

Hedgehog Helpers Unite............................122

Gardener's Friend 130

Hedgehog Highways and Byways.............142

Get Your Paws Dirty...................................150

Spotted a Hedgehog?
Here's What to Do 170

Hedgehog Heroes 178

Test Your Hog Knowledge.........................182

Your Hog-Friendly Garden Checklist........184

INTRODUCTION

Why We Love Hedgehogs

After a long day, there's something enchanting about coming into the garden and hearing the quiet rustle of leaves at dusk. Then, if you're lucky, you spot it: a hedgehog, snuffling its way through the undergrowth.

With its twitching snout, careful waddle, and tiny, determined steps, a hedgehog can make even the smallest garden feel magical and full of possibility. They may be covered in thousands of spines, but hedgehogs are unquestionably adorable and impossible not to love!

INTRODUCTION

For generations, hedgehogs have remained a comforting symbol of British wildlife at its most wondrous and fascinating. Beloved in children's stories and celebrated in countless outdoor ornaments, these small creatures have quietly shared our gardens, parks and hedgerows for centuries – keeping nature in balance by hoovering up slugs, beetles, and other pests, as well as reminding us to appreciate the wild world right on our doorstep. Few animals capture our hearts and collective imagination quite like the hedgehog.

But in recent years, those quiet, moonlit visits have grown rarer, and the hedgehog's future in Britain is far less secure than its place in our hearts. Once a familiar sight in gardens and hedgerows, their numbers have plummeted in recent decades. In the 1950s, the UK's hedgehog population was estimated at around 30 million, but today it has fallen to fewer than 900,000. We've now reached the heart-breaking point where hedgehogs are considered vulnerable to extinction.

I HEART HEDGEHOGS

For a woodland creature that roams the night in search of food and shelter, the modern world – with its busy roads, tidy gardens, and disappearing wild spaces – has made survival more challenging than ever before.

That's why hedgehogs need a helping hand and there's so much we can do to help them thrive. It doesn't take much: a small gap in a fence, a dish of water, or a patch of leaves left undisturbed can make all the difference. With a bit of care and attention, we can ensure that Britain's most beloved garden guest remains part of our nights for generations to come.

In this book, we'll invite you to step into the world of the hedgehog – to discover their special habits, their place in myth and folklore, and their enduring presence in culture. You'll also find practical tips to make your garden or local green space hedgehog-friendly and help keep these treasured animals safe.

So, let's open the garden gate and step quietly into their world. It's a world worth protecting – and once you've peeked inside, no corner of the garden will ever seem ordinary again.

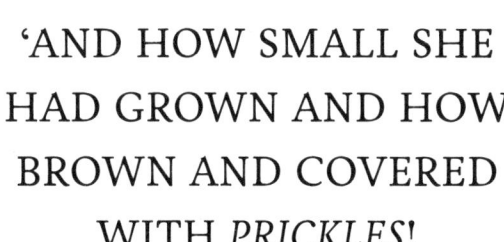

'AND HOW SMALL SHE HAD GROWN AND HOW BROWN AND COVERED WITH *PRICKLES*!

WHY!
MRS. TIGGY-WINKLE WAS NOTHING BUT A *HEDGEHOG!*'

Beatrix Potter,
The Tale of Mrs. Tiggy-Winkle

GET TO KNOW YOUR HEDGEHOG

Hedgehog 101

In this chapter, we'll meet the tiny, spiky creature whose story stretches back millions and millions of years. Get to know all about the hedgehog under all those prickles and dive into all the charming little traits that make this animal so unique.

ANCIENT AND ADORABLE: The story of the hedgehog

If you really want to get to know the hedgehog, you'll need to travel *way* back in time – millions of years, in fact. Hedgehog-like animals are believed to have first appeared around 56 to 34 million years ago, during the Eocene period, when the Earth was cooling and grasslands were starting to spread. But fossils of a spiky mammal discovered in Spain reveal that hedgehogs may have been around for as much as 125 million years. Now that's one ancient little creature.

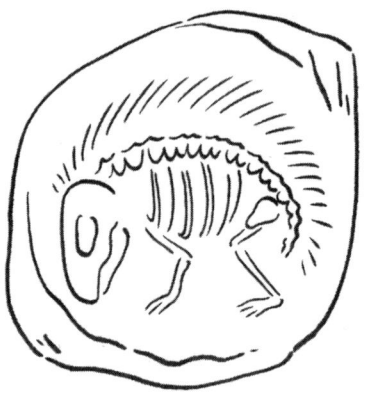

GET TO KNOW YOUR HEDGEHOG

Archaeologists have also discovered hedgehog remains at ancient sites across Britain, showing that these adorable animals have been in this country for at least half a million years. At Stonehenge, a child's grave from the late Bronze or early Iron Age was even found with what is believed to be a tiny chalk hedgehog figurine – affectionately nicknamed the 'Hengehog'. Archaeologists think it may be the earliest known depiction of a hedgehog in human history.

And you know what's really amazing? Fossil records show that hedgehogs from those ancient times look almost identical to the ones we see today. Since the age of the mammoths, they've hardly changed at all – proof that when you're this perfectly designed, there's no need to evolve!

I HEART HEDGEHOGS

THE HEDGEHOG MULTIVERSE

Did you know there are 17 species of hedgehogs roaming across Europe, Asia and Africa? Most of them sport five adorable toes on each foot, though the 'four-toed hedgehog' decided to do its own thing – literally missing a toe! From the 'long-eared hedgehog' with its comically oversized ears built for desert life, to the 'Indian hedgehog', whose striped face makes it look a bit like a tiny badger, each species has its own individual charm.

The 'North African hedgehog' is a speedy little runner, while the 'desert hedgehog' stays cool with shorter spines and a lighter coat. The tiny 'African pygmy hedgehog' is a favourite among pet lovers. But in the UK, it's the charming 'European hedgehog' that is commonly seen – the snuffling garden visitor we all know and love.

'THE HEDGEHOG IS ONE OF BRITAIN'S GREATEST NATURAL CURIOSITIES.'

David Attenborough

THE HEDGEHOG BLUEPRINT

Hedgehogs may be small, but they're brilliantly built. These little mammals have short, strong legs and big clawed feet that are perfect for digging and scurrying around. Their fur-covered bodies are usually brown or black. But on the island of Alderney in the Channel Islands, something unusual happens – around 25 per cent of the hedgehogs there are blonde! This rare colouring comes from a genetic condition called leucism, which causes pale skin and creamy-coloured spines.

Adult hedgehogs range in size from about 14 to 30 centimetres long and usually weigh just 450 to 900 grams. They are truly pocket-sized creatures. Most people don't realise hedgehogs also have a teeny tiny tail, only about 1 to 2 centimetres long, which is usually hidden underneath.

No hedgehog would be complete without its cute pig-like snout and tiny rounded ears. But of course, what really sets them apart is the forest of spines that covers their back. These spines are what make a hedgehog unmistakably, wonderfully and entirely unique.

GET TO KNOW YOUR HEDGEHOG

HOG TRIVIA: An adult hedgehog has around 34 to 44 teeth. That is more than a human. The average adult human usually only has around 32 teeth.

'THE FOX HAS MANY TRICKS. THE HEDGEHOG HAS BUT ONE, BUT THAT IS THE BEST OF ALL.'

Archilochus

GET TO KNOW YOUR HEDGEHOG

SMALL BUT SPIKY

There's no mistaking a hedgehog – those spines are its signature look. They may seem cute and harmless, but underneath that enchanting exterior lies one of nature's cleverest bits of armour.

An adult hedgehog has around 5,000 to 7,000 spines, each one a tiny engineering marvel. These short, stiff hairs are made of keratin (the same stuff as our hair and nails) and are built for defence.

Each spine is about 2.5 to 3 centimetres long and connected to its own little muscle, so the hedgehog can raise or lower them in an instant. When danger is near, up they go, turning the hedgehog into a prickly fortress that's almost impossible to bite.

Hedgehogs do not have a traditional fight or flight response. But if a predator gets too close, the hedgehog does have one glorious trick – it curls into a perfect, spiny ball! A special muscle wraps around its little body like a drawstring, pulling everything in and sealing off its soft tummy, face and legs. Even if a hedgehog takes a tumble while in this defensive ball shape, those spines act like built-in shock absorbers, softening the fall. Clever hog.

I HEART HEDGEHOGS

Baby hedgehogs (known as 'hoglets') are born with soft, pale spines hidden under their skin – thankfully for mum. Within hours of being born, those spines emerge and soon harden as they grow. And just like humans shed hair, hedgehogs regularly lose and replace their spines in a process called quilling – keeping their armour fresh, sharp, and ready for anything.

GET TO KNOW YOUR HEDGEHOG

SWEET SIXTEEN

The world's oldest known hedgehog, a European hedgehog named Thorvald from Denmark, lived an impressive 16 years. Before Thorvald, the record-holder was a 9-year-old female hedgehog discovered in Ireland.

Scientists can actually tell a hedgehog's age by studying its jawbone. 'You can tell the age of a hedgehog by counting growth rings in their jawbones, like you would on trees,' Danish researcher Sophie Lund Rasmussen told the BBC.

However, making it to your sweet sixteen as a hedgehog is a rare feat. In the wild, most hedgehogs only make it to about 2 or 3 years old. Facing a host of modern dangers – from predators and traffic to limited food – few hedgehogs in Britain survive beyond their second birthday.

WHO HUNTS THE HEDGEHOG?

In the UK, few animals prey on the European hedgehog. Badgers are their main natural predator, which are strong enough to tackle even an adult hedgehog despite its spines. Foxes might attack but often give up quickly once they realise the hedgehog's spines are too much trouble.

Young hedgehogs are more vulnerable and can be taken by owls, magpies, or crows. Occasionally, dogs will injure them as well. Still, the biggest threat isn't from predators – it's from people. Cars, garden hazards, and loss of habitat cause far more harm to the hedgehog than any wild animal.

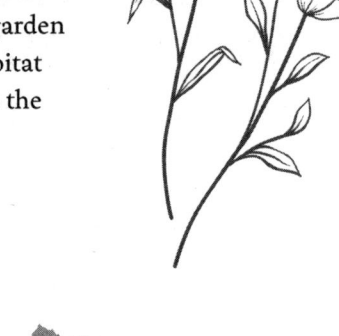

'A HEDGEHOGGE SEEMES TO BE BUT A POORE SILLY CREATURE, NOT LIKELY TO DOE ANY GREAT HARME, YET INDEEDE IT IS FULL OF BRISTLES OR PRICKLES, WHEREBY IT MAY ANNOY A MAN VERY SHREWDLY.'

Thomas Playfere

'THE HEDGEHOG WAS ENGAGED IN A FIGHT WITH ANOTHER HEDGEHOG, WHICH SEEMED TO ALICE AN EXCELLENT OPPORTUNITY FOR CROQUETING ONE OF THEM WITH THE OTHER.'

Lewis Carroll,
Alice in Wonderland

GET TO KNOW YOUR HEDGEHOG

NOT A PORCUPINE!

Hedgehogs sometimes get nicknamed 'the British porcupine'. But even though hedgehogs might look like mini porcupines, they're not related to them at all.

For one thing, hedgehog spines are short, smooth, and firmly attached – they don't shoot out or stick into anyone. Porcupine quills, on the other hand, are long, barbed, and can detach on contact. Ouch!

Hedgehogs are also far smaller than porcupines and spend their nights hunting insects and slugs, while porcupines are hefty plant-eaters with a taste for bark and leaves. And, unlike hedgehogs, porcupines never made it to Britain at all.

In fact, the hedgehog's closest relatives are shrews – tiny insect-eaters with no spines whatsoever. The common shrew has a pointy nose, minuscule eyes, and a turbo-charged metabolism that means it must eat every 2 to 3 hours. You might even spot a shrew darting through your garden – a distant cousin of the hedgehog minus the prickles.

THE SECRET LIFE OF HEDGEHOGS

What they get up to when no one's looking

When we're winding down for the night – brushing our teeth, fluffing our pillows, switching off the bedside lamp – the humble hedgehog is just clocking in for work. As darkness settles, these little creatures come alive, setting out on their nightly wanderings.

Hedgehogs are truly nocturnal. By around 11 o'clock at night, hedgehogs are in full swing and on the hunt for dinner. Let's find out what these little cuties get up to when no one else is looking.

"'RATHER!' REPLIED THE OTTER, WINKING AT THE MOLE. "THE SIGHT OF THESE GREEDY YOUNG HEDGEHOGS STUFFING THEMSELVES WITH FRIED HAM MAKES ME FEEL POSITIVELY FAMISHED."

THE HEDGEHOGS, WHO WERE JUST BEGINNING TO FEEL HUNGRY AGAIN AFTER THEIR PORRIDGE, AND AFTER WORKING SO HARD AT THEIR FRYING, LOOKED TIMIDLY UP AT MR. BADGER, BUT WERE TOO SHY TO SAY ANYTHING.'

Kenneth Grahame,
The Wind in the Willows

MIDNIGHT MUNCHIES

As night falls, hedgehogs get busy rummaging through the dark for food – which begs the question: what do hedgehogs actually eat in the wild?

Well, hedgehogs are true opportunists when it comes to food – meaning that they will quite literally eat anything. They're omnivores, meaning they'll happily tuck into both plants and animals. Their favourites? Juicy beetles, worms, caterpillars, slugs and snails. Every so often, they'll snack on a fallen bird's egg or a frog. In towns, they've even been known to sneak a bite of cat or dog food left on the doorstep.

However, hedgehogs are primarily insectivores. Around 70 per cent of their diet comes from invertebrates. This appetite for bugs makes them a gardener's best friend, quietly helping to keep pests under control. With hedgehogs around, your plants are less likely to be devoured by slugs and caterpillars, letting your garden flourish naturally.

Water is also essential for hedgehogs. In the wild, hedgehogs sip from dew, puddles and ponds.

HOG TRIVIA: Hedgehogs have more than a metre of intestines and they also possess a massive stomach for their tiny size. As a result, a hedgehog can eat up to one-third of its body weight in one night. Imagine eating that much chocolate in an evening – we'd never move again! These tiny hedgehogs are also very noisy eaters, snuffling, grunting and crunching their way as they forage for their next meal.

STRONG STOMACHS

A hedgehog's digestion is not for the faint-hearted. Hedgehogs can stomach just about anything – even venom! They've been known to gobble down the poisonous Spanish fly beetle and survive snake bites. One rather daring hedgehog in Orpington, Greater London was reportedly spotted licking sulphuric acid from a car battery (don't try that at home, of course).

THE MILK MYTH

Gardeners love hedgehogs because they gobble up all the slugs, snails and other pests that plague our gardens. But the traditional saucer of bread and milk that well-meaning hedgehog fans leave out might not be so great for the hogs themselves. Despite their legendary stomachs, milk and bread have very little nutritional value for hedgehogs and can even make these little lactose-intolerant animals very sick. Find out exactly what you can and can't feed hedgehogs on page 162.

HOME BEFORE DAWN

After a long night's feast, most hedgehogs shuffle back to their nests by around 3 o'clock in the morning. Some hedgehogs might stay out until 5 or 6 a.m., but soon enough, even they're curling up to sleep the day away in a cosy nest of leaves and grass.

THE NIGHT AND THE DAY SHIFT

If you spot a hedgehog during daylight, it's usually a hungry mother looking for food while caring for her babies. Find out when you should help a hedgehog on page 170.

'IF I PASS DURING SOME NOCTURNAL BLACKNESS, MOTHY AND WARM, WHEN THE HEDGEHOG TRAVELS FURTIVELY OVER THE LAWN.'

Thomas Hardy,
'Afterwards'

LITTLE CREATURES, BIG TALENTS

Beneath those prickles lies a world of hidden talents and quirky habits most of us never see. From impressive senses and surprising speed to mysterious self-anointing rituals, hedgehogs have a whole secret set of skills and attributes waiting to be discovered ...

QUICK ON THEIR FEET
They may look like tiny wind-up toys when they waddle along, but don't be fooled – hedgehogs can really move fast when they need to. Hidden beneath that round body are surprisingly long legs that can carry them at speeds of up to 6 mph (about 10 km/h). If you ever get to see one running, you might be shocked at just how quick and long-legged they are.

FLOATING ON SPINES
Hedgehogs aren't just land lovers – they're strong swimmers too. They can paddle across surprisingly wide rivers, sometimes covering up to half a mile. Their hollow, air-filled spines even help them float, so if they

get tired mid-swim, they can roll onto their backs and drift like they're lying on a built-in Lilo.

Swimming is often part of their nightly foraging routine. So, if they catch the scent of food on the far bank, they'll plunge right in. But while hedgehogs are good swimmers, many sadly drown in garden ponds and swimming pools each year – a reminder to make your garden a little hedgehog-friendlier (you can find out how on page 130).

SELF-ANOINTING LITTLE WEIRDOS

When a hedgehog comes across something with a strong smell – like a toad's skin, poisonous plants, or even animal droppings – it gets to work. It chews the substance, makes a frothy saliva, and then spreads it all over its spines. No one knows for sure why they do it. But it could be to disguise their scent from predators or to coat their spines with a touch of toxin for extra defence. Strange behaviour, but very hedgehog.

I HEART HEDGEHOGS

NIGHT OWLS WITH POOR EYESIGHT

Hedgehogs come alive after dark, but their eyesight leaves a lot to be desired. They can't see far, struggle with depth perception, and often bump into stuff. Poor things!

SUPER SNIFFERS AND SHARP LISTENERS

What hedgehogs lack in eyesight, they more than make up for with their nose and ears. Their sense of smell is so strong they can detect a beetle or an earthworm buried several centimetres underground. They also have incredible hearing and are super sensitive to sound. Scientists have noticed that hedgehogs flinch when they hear keys jingling or people clicking their tongues, suggesting they can pick up high-pitched noises beyond our hearing range.

MIDNIGHT MARATHONERS

Once darkness falls, hedgehogs set off on long nightly walks in search of food and company. They usually travel a kilometre or two each night, but can go even farther if needed. Every evening's route is an adventure filled with sniffing, munching and exploring.

THE SECRET LIFE OF HEDGEHOGS

LONERS BY NATURE

Hedgehogs are true solo travellers. They prefer their own company and rarely spend time with other hedgehogs outside of mating season. Research suggests that hedgehogs may even avoid one another on purpose – using scent cues to make sure they don't cross paths or compete for the same food.

NOISY NEIGHBOURS

For such small creatures, hedgehogs are surprisingly loud. They have a whole range of sounds – grunts, squeals, hisses and snuffles – each with its own meaning. Adults tend to get vocal when they're excited or alarmed, while babies whistle or chirp to get their mother's attention.

I HEART HEDGEHOGS

Here's what those sounds usually mean:

GRUNTING AND SNUFFLING: A hedgehog on the move, busily hunting for food.

CHUFFING: That rhythmic puffing sound means love is in the air – it's part of the hedgehog courtship ritual.

CHIRPING: Hungry hoglets calling from the nest.

SCREAMING: A distress call – the hedgehog is hurt or frightened.

HISSING: A clear warning to back off.

CLICKING OR POPPING: A challenge, often between rival males during mating season.

'THE HEDGEHOG WAS STANDING BEFORE HIS DOOR WITH HIS ARMS CROSSED, HUMMING A LITTLE SONG TO HIMSELF, NEITHER BETTER NOR WORSE THAN HEDGEHOGS USUALLY SING ON A NICE SUNDAY MORNING.'

Jacob and Wilhelm Grimm,
'The Hare and the Hedgehog'

A YEAR IN THE LIFE OF A HEDGEHOG

Hedgehogs may look sleepy and unassuming, but their lives follow a fascinating annual rhythm. Here's what a typical hedgehog year looks like.

THE SECRET LIFE OF HEDGEHOGS

Winter Slumber (January – February)
Through the chill of winter, hedgehogs lie in deep hibernation, safely tucked away in leaf piles, compost heaps or log shelters. They conserve every bit of energy, only stirring briefly during mild spells before returning to their cosy nests until spring.

Waking up to Spring (March – April)
As the days grow longer and the air warms, hedgehogs begin to wake. Groggy and hungry, they set off in search of much-needed food. Males emerge first, claiming territories and preparing for the busy breeding season ahead.

The Season of Love (May – June)
Spring turns to summer, and the hedgehog breeding season (the 'rut') is in full swing. Males travel far and wide in search of females, sometimes circling them in noisy courtship displays. Once mating is done, the males move on, while females build snug summer nests ready for their young.

I HEART HEDGEHOGS

New Beginnings (July – August)
Tiny hoglets – usually four or five per litter – are born. For the first few weeks, they stay safely in the nest, feeding on their mother's milk before joining her on short night-time foraging trips. By 6 to 8 weeks old, the youngsters become independent.

Preparing for the Cold (September – October)
As autumn sets in, hedgehogs focus on two important jobs: feeding and building. They forage constantly, visiting gardens and feeding stations to pack on fat for the winter. At the same time, they construct their hibernation nests, which are essential for surviving the cold months ahead.

Settling in for Winter (November – December)
As food dwindles and the cold sets in, hedgehogs retreat into their specially made nests and settle into hibernation. Hedgehogs can hibernate for up to 4 months at a time if they need to conserve energy. So, from November until the end of February, they sleep deeply, relying on their stored fat to survive until spring returns – beginning the cycle anew.

HEDGEHOG HOME SWEET HOME

Hedgehogs are surprisingly discerning when it comes to their real estate. These clever little property managers often keep several homely nests on the go – sometimes as many as ten. Hedgehogs choose which nest to use depending on the weather, food availability, or safety from predators. Each nest is carefully chosen and built to suit the season and the hedgehog's needs.

They have three main types of nests, each serving a special purpose:

Summer Nests
Simple and cosy, these are hedgehogs' daytime hideaways during the warmer months. Often made from tufts of long grass, dry leaves or moss, they're built in quiet corners – beneath shrubs, in compost heaps or tucked away in overgrown areas. Hedgehogs use them to rest safely while remaining close to good foraging grounds.

Nursery Nests

Built by mother hedgehogs in late spring or early summer, these are sturdy, well-insulated structures designed to keep the litter warm and dry. Females use layers of leaves, grasses and moss woven tightly together to form a waterproof dome. Nursery nests are usually tucked under dense vegetation, garden sheds or hedgerows, keeping curious predators away while the baby hedgehogs grow strong enough to venture out.

Winter Hibernation Nests (Hibernacula)

These are the palaces of hedgehog life. Constructed in autumn, winter hibernation nests or 'hibernacula' are thick, multi-layered shelters made from dry leaves, twigs, reeds and grass, built in secluded, frost-free spots such as under hedges, bramble thickets, log piles or sheds. A well-made hibernaculum can be remarkably weatherproof, keeping the hedgehog snug and protected from cold, wind and rain during months of deep sleep.

'A HEDGEHOG CURLS HIMSELF UP INTO A BALL AND HIS PRICKLES STICK OUT EVERY WHICH WAY AT ONCE. BY THIS YOU MAY KNOW THE HEDGEHOG.'

Rudyard Kipling,
'The Beginning of the Armadillos',
Just So Stories

PRICKLY PASSIONS:
The secret love life of hedgehogs

Hedgehogs are mostly solitary creatures. They roam, feed, and explore on their own, only coming together during the breeding season to mate. And when the breeding season arrives, they become surprisingly sociable, meeting multiple partners and making quite a ruckus. It's almost like a hedgehog house party.

> HOG TRIVIA: The rarely used collective noun for hedgehogs is an 'array' or 'prickle'. How cute!

COURTSHIP CHAOS

Hedgehog courtship happens in spring and summer, with May and June being the busiest rut. Male hedgehogs put on quite the show to win over a female partner. They will spend hours circling a female, while she makes loud huffing and puffing sounds.

The commotion can attract rival males. Head-butting, chasing, and even rolling each other out of the way are normal behaviours as males compete for mates. It may look brutal to human eyes, but it's just part of hedgehog hot-girl summer.

HOW LOVE HAPPENS

When a female hedgehog accepts a male, the actual process of mating is a delicate operation, given the female has 5,000 spines to contend with! The female adopts a special body position where she flattens her body and presses her spines down, as the male mounts from behind.

Both male and female hedgehogs are promiscuous, often mating with multiple partners throughout the season. If a mother successfully raises her first litter, she may even have a second one with a different male hedgehog later in the summer.

INDEPENDENT HOGS

Hedgehogs reach sexual maturity in their second year and after that, they can breed every year until the end of their lives. But male hedgehogs provide no parental care and usually leave after mating – moving on to find the next female partner. Hedgehogs do not pair bond and the female will raise her young unaided by the male.

NOISES IN THE NIGHT

The rut isn't quiet! Males circling females and rival males squaring up can create a surprising amount of racket in your garden. If you hear strange snorts, huffs or puffs during this time of year, it could very well be hedgehogs in mating season!

ALL ABOUT HOGLETS

Little baby hoglets are the adorable results of hedgehogs' secretive love lives. After a gestation period of around 35 to 58 days, the hoglets are born, weighing, on average, just 15 grams. Litter sizes vary but the typical hedgehog litter has an average of four to five hoglets.

A BABY'S FIRST SPINES

At birth, the tiny hoglets are blind and look a bit like soft white caterpillars! Their soft, flexible spines are protected by a fluid-filled skin, so mum isn't hurt during birth. Within a day, this skin shrinks and sheds, revealing around 150 new spines.

MAMA KNOWS BEST

For the first few weeks, the mother hedgehog is the sole provider. Mummy hedgehog will lie on her side, allowing the rows of hoglets to feed. Hoglets start competing for milk around 1 week old, pushing and shoving for the best spots. The mother keeps a watchful eye, especially on other male hedgehogs who may pose a threat. By about a month, the little ones have dense, dark spines and their eyes are open.

FIRST ADVENTURES

As we have learned, hedgehogs are independent, solitary souls, and hoglets start their own journey pretty quickly. At around 4 weeks, hoglets begin following mum on foraging trips outside the nest, learning the ropes of hedgehog life. By 6 to 8 weeks, they're ready to leave the nest and venture out independently. At this point, they weigh roughly 250 grams (which is about the same weight as an apple) and start claiming their own little territories – maybe under a terrace or in a woodpile. There, they build their own nests and start the cycle all over again.

NAMELESS LITTLES

Until the 1990s, there wasn't even a proper word for baby hedgehogs! Nowadays, hoglet (or sometimes 'hedgehoglet') is used to describe these tiny, spiny bundles of joy. Before they got their official name in the 1990s, they were commonly called pups, kits and even piglets.

TOUGH CHOICES

Life as a hedgehog mother can be brutal. If food is scarce, or the nest is too crowded, she may eat some of her hoglets so the rest have a better chance of survival. It's a harsh strategy, but one shaped by nature to give her babies the best odds.

I HEART HEDGEHOGS

Mum may also do this if the nest is disturbed. She might decide that if predators are threatening her babies, it's safer to eat them herself than risk them being eaten anyway. Or stress might simply overwhelm her, and she abandons the nest to start fresh somewhere safer. It's a stark reminder that hedgehogs live in a world where survival sometimes means making very hard decisions.

'IF YOU START THROWING HEDGEHOGS UNDER ME, I SHALL THROW A COUPLE OF PORCUPINES UNDER YOU.'

Nikita Khrushchev

I HEART HEDGEHOGS

HEDGEHOGS IN WINTER MODE

THE SECRET LIFE OF HEDGEHOGS

Hedgehogs are Britain's only prickly mammals and also one of the few true hibernators around. Those nifty little spines offer almost no protection against the cold, so when winter arrives, hedgehogs curl up in cosy nests made from layered leaves in sheltered spots and sleep through the chilly months. From November to March, when insects and other favourite foods are scarce, they hunker down and conserve energy.

Like all animals, hedgehogs need energy to grow, move and survive. Their food fuels them, but when temperatures drop and meals are hard to find, they slow their metabolism to stretch what energy they have. During hibernation, their bodies slow dramatically: heart rates drop from around 190 beats per minute to just 20; body temperatures fall from 35°C to 10°C or lower; and they breathe only once every few minutes. Every process in their bodies slows, helping them survive the winter with minimal energy until food and warmer weather return.

While hibernating, hedgehogs only wake briefly – about every 11 days. They rarely leave their nests, and these arousals last a day or two. Sometimes these wake-ups happen for no reason. In other cases, a disturbance or unexpectedly warm spell prompts them to stir. These short awakenings let hedgehogs check that their nests are still intact and help them sense when spring has arrived and it's safe to return to the outside world. Hedgehogs will emerge when night-time temperatures consistently stay above 5°C. By the time they finish hibernating, they may have lost up to 40 per cent of their body weight.

When spring finally arrives, hedgehogs shake off the long winter slumber and get back to their busy little lives in the outside world. They wander through gardens and hedgerows in search of tasty treats, exploring, and of course enjoying a little spring romance (or two!). After months of snoozing in their snug nests, we might just be lucky enough to catch a glimpse of a hedgehog in the wild.

THE UNIQUE PLACES WHERE HEDGEHOGS LIVE AROUND THE WORLD

Not all hedgehog species inhabit gardens and woodlands. These little explorers have made homes in some of the most surprising and unusual places on Earth.

The Saharan Desert

The desert hedgehog manages to survive in the Saharan desert – one of the hottest and driest places on the planet. Found across North Africa and the Arabian Peninsula too, the desert hedgehog lives near oases and dry riverbeds where food and shade are easier to find. During the day, it hides underground or even buries itself in the sand to stay cool. When night falls, the desert hedgehog comes out to hunt insects. It's proof that the desert life isn't just for camels and lizards.

I HEART HEDGEHOGS

The Ancient Ruins of Rome
Among the crumbling ruins of Rome, Italy, European hedgehogs have found an unexpected urban paradise. They wander through the city's old palace grounds, archaeological sites, and green corridors that link the countryside to the heart of Rome. These connected patches of nature act like safe highways, helping hedgehogs move around freely even in a bustling capital.

In Italy, these hedgehogs are protected by law (it's illegal to keep them as pets) and these animals have become a small but important part of Rome's ecosystem. There's even a special rescue centre nearby called 'La Ninna', that helps injured hedgehogs get back on their feet.

The Dry Plains of India and Pakistan
In the open plains and sandy deserts of India and Pakistan, the Indian hedgehog lives its signature solitary life. The Indian hedgehog doesn't hibernate, but when food is hard to find, it cleverly slows down its metabolism to save energy.

New Zealand's Forests and Gardens

When European settlers brought hedgehogs to New Zealand in the 1870s, they thought the animals would help control garden pests. Instead, the hedgehogs found paradise. With no foxes or badgers to hunt them, they spread quickly across the country.

Unfortunately, hedgehogs now eat the native insects, lizards and bird eggs in New Zealand, with the country's conservationists warning that the animals have become a serious threat to local wildlife and a pest in their own right.

The Deserts and Steppes of the Middle East and Central Asia

From Egypt and Turkey to Mongolia and China, the long-eared hedgehog lives in dry, open landscapes where few animals can survive. Its huge ears help it stay cool by releasing heat. The long-eared hedgehog is also a quick runner and expert digger.

HOGS IN HISTORY AND FOLKLORE

Myths, legends and their starring roles in books and art

We might think of hedgehogs as gentle, prickly little wanderers of our gardens, but they haven't always had such a sweet reputation. In fact, for centuries, these spiny creatures were caught up in a tangle of superstition, suspicion and downright fear. Once linked to witches, accused of stealing milk from cows, and even hunted as vermin, hedgehogs were far from the adored icons of British wildlife we know today.

In this chapter, we'll take a journey through their fascinating history, exploring how hedgehogs went from maligned and feared creatures to the cherished, whimsical emblem of the British countryside. Along the way, we'll discover just why the hedgehog has earned its place in the hearts of so many – including ours!

WHAT'S IN A NAME?

These spiky little sweethearts weren't always called hedgehogs. Back in the medieval times, they were known as 'urchins'.

And back then, the word urchin didn't just mean a hedgehog – it also meant goblins and elves. And medieval people once believed that these magical creatures could transform into hedgehogs.

By the mid-1400s, people started using the word urchin for the spiky marine creature we now call the sea urchin instead – because it just looked so much like a little hedgehog. Around the same time in the fifteenth century, the word 'heggehogge' started to be used to refer to our favourite animals – 'hegge' for the hedgerows they love to snuffle through, and 'hogge' for their cute, pig-like snouts.

HOGS IN HISTORY AND FOLKLORE

HOG TRIVIA: The Irish word for hedgehog is 'gainneog', which roughly translates to 'ugly little thing'. By contrast, in Germany, hedgehogs get a much sweeter treatment: the word 'igelschnäuzchen' is a term of endearment, meaning 'little hedgehog snout'. Awww.

I HEART HEDGEHOGS

SHAKESPEARE'S SPIKY INSULTS

Believe it or not, hedgehogs got a rough rap in some of Shakespeare's greatest plays. These humble creatures appear four times in Shakespeare's works, usually as a term implying discomfort – or as a not-so-gentle insult. In *Richard III*, Anne snaps at Richard: 'Dost grant me, hedgehog? Then, God grant me too; Thou mayst be damned for that wicked deed!' Not exactly a compliment.

In *Macbeth*, one of the witches includes the 'hedge-pig' in her spell: 'Thrice and once the hedge-pig whined,' showing just how closely hedgehogs were tied to mischief and witchcraft historically.

In *A Midsummer Night's Dream*, Shakespeare lines them up with a whole host of other unpleasant creatures: 'You spotted snakes with double tongue, Thorny hedgehogs, not be seen; Newts and blindworms, do no wrong; Come not near our Fairy Queen.'

Meanwhile, in *The Tempest*, Shakespeare captures both the literal and figurative prickliness of hedgehogs when Caliban complains of the hedgehogs: 'which Lie tumbling in my barefoot way and mount Their pricks at my footfall.' Shakespeare certainly wasn't a fan, but we know these animals are far more endearing than he gave them credit for.

'DOST GRANT ME, HEDGEHOG?'

William Shakespeare, *Richard III*

'HE LIES LIKE A HEDGEHOG ROLL'D UP THE WRONG WAY, TORMENTING HIMSELF WITH HIS PRICKLES.'

Thomas Hood, 'Her Dream'

WITCHES, OMENS AND APPLE COLLECTORS

Not so long ago, hedgehogs didn't enjoy the friendly reputation they have today. Far from being seen as endearing garden visitors, they were once regarded with mistrust and unease – creatures to be wary of rather than welcomed.

Back in the Middle Ages, spotting a hedgehog was considered seriously bad luck. In Christian folklore, hedgehogs symbolised sin and selfishness – creatures that curled into themselves, keeping everything hidden. Medieval people thought these animals were witches in disguise and these witches would shapeshift into hedgehogs. So that prickly little figure in the hedgerow? Supposedly, it might have been a witch sneaking about to cause mischief!

Even the Ancient Romans had their own ideas. Pliny the Elder (a Roman author and naturalist who loved collecting curious tales about the natural world) claimed that hedgehogs rolled on grapes and apples to carry them home on their spines. The story stuck around for centuries, and by the Middle Ages people across Europe genuinely believed hedgehogs raided orchards at night, stealing fruit and hoarding it for winter.

This image of the crafty little fruit thief found its way into medieval fables, art and folklore, turning the poor hedgehog into a symbol of slyness and mischief. (In truth, hedgehogs walk with their spines flat, so the only thing they could 'collect' would be a few stray leaves at best!)

But nonetheless, our beloved hedgehog became the spiky little scapegoat for all sorts of human fears and tall tales.

'HIS MEATE IS APPLES, WORMES, OR GRAPES; WHEN HE FINDETH APPLES OR GRAPES ON THE EARTH, HEE ROWLETH HIMSELFE UPPON THEM, UNTILL HE HAVE FILLED ALL HIS PRICKLES, AND THEN CARRIETH THEM HOME TO HIS DEN, NEVER BEARING ABOVE ONE IN HIS MOUTH. [...] SO FOORTH HEE GOETH, MAKING A NOYSE LIKE A CART WHEALE.'

Edward Topsell,
Historie of Four-Footed Beasts

WANTED! HEDGEHOGS: Milk thieves on the loose!

Just when you thought it couldn't get worse, along came one of history's strangest rumours: the idea that hedgehogs snuck into barns at night to steal milk straight from cows' udders.

Yes, really. For centuries in England and Ireland, people believed hedgehogs – or witches disguised as them – were responsible for cows not producing any milk. Professor of Witchcraft, Owen Davies, told the BBC that for many centuries, hedgehogs were 'widely thought to suck the udders of cows, leaving the cows dry in the morning'. Never mind that hedgehogs are lactose intolerant and would be terrified by the idea of a midnight dairy raid!

The milk-stealing myth spread so widely that it reached the highest levels of British government. By the 1500s, hedgehogs were officially classed as 'vermin' and it led to the poor creatures being almost hunted to extinction. King Henry VIII's government even offered bounties for every hedgehog killed under the 1539

HOGS IN HISTORY AND FOLKLORE

Preservation of Grain Act. In 1566, Queen Elizabeth I bolstered the original bill and the statute – setting a price of two pence per hedgehog head. That was twice as much as the bounty for a wildcat at the time.

Over the following centuries, hundreds of thousands of bounties were paid out, all because people believed hedgehogs were stealing milk. It's heartbreaking – and absurd – to think a creature now loved for its charm and shyness was once hunted down for imagined crimes it couldn't possibly commit.

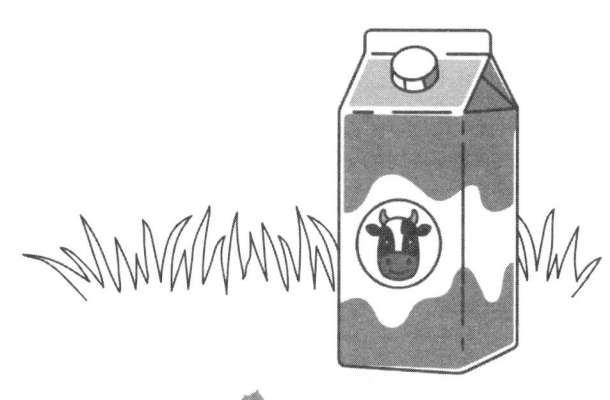

HEDGEHOGS IN THE HOUSEHOLD

Long before they became beloved garden visitors, hedgehogs had rather practical uses.

The Ancient Romans actually used hedgehog skins – covered in spines – to clean their clothes. They became so popular in the household that the Roman Senate had to regulate the trade in hedgehog skins. The Ancient Romans also used hedgehog spines to train animals, like stopping calves from suckling after weaning.

By the Middle Ages, people were still finding creative – and slightly alarming – ways to use hedgehogs. Their spines made handy brushes and dissecting pins, and their meat was even used in medieval medicine. Some believed hedgehog parts could treat everything from colic to baldness (spoiler: they couldn't).

> 'HE MAKES A NEST
> AND FILLS IT FULL
> OF FRUIT,
> ON THE HEDGE
> BOTTOM HUNTS FOR
> CRABS AND SLOES
> AND WHISTLES
> LIKE A CRICKET
> AS HE GOES.'

John Clare,
'The Hedgehog'

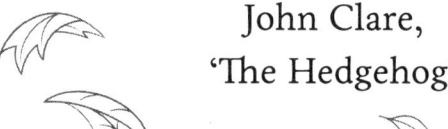

THE HEDGEHOG'S PRACTICAL PAST

These were some of the most popular practical uses for hedgehogs in history.

WOOL CARE: Hedgehog skins were stretched over wood and used to card raw wool before spinning. Carding is the process used to align and clean raw wool fibres so they can be spun into yarn. Hedgehog spines were also used to fluff up woollen garments and remove tangles from wool cloth.

HAIR AND SKIN REMEDIES: Among some Romany communities and in Morocco, hedgehog blood was traditionally used as a cure for cracked skin, warts and ringworm.

HOGS IN HISTORY AND FOLKLORE

ODD BALDNESS CURES: In Ancient Egypt and Classical times, people rubbed a mix of ground spines or hedgehog oil on the skin to treat baldness. Later, a seventeenth-century English text recommended hedgehog faeces for baldness!

MEDICAL BELIEFS: An eighteenth-century folk remedy suggested drinking a mix of roasted, powdered hedgehog skin to help kidney stones. Older British traditions included eating cooked hedgehog to treat fits. Other supposed remedies suggested eating the left eye of a hedgehog to strengthen weak eyes, or the jawbone to cure rheumatism.

HEDGEHOG ON A SPIT

But the most surprising thing? People actually ate hedgehogs. Hedgehog roasting is, historically, a real tradition among Romany people. The little creatures are rolled in clay and cooked over open campfires. When the clay cracks away, it pulls the spines right off – leaving the hedgehog exposed, ready for eating.

The eighteenth-century chef John Farley even included hedgehog recipes in *The London Art of Cookery*, suggesting they be served with almonds. Some said hedgehog meat tasted like pork, although the poet John Clare called it 'black and bitter and unsavoury'.

Even in modern times, the hedgehog has popped up in culinary oddities. In the early 2000s, British roadkill chef Arthur Boyt reportedly cooked a hedgehog spaghetti carbonara. And in the 1980s, inventor Philip Lewis released 'Hedgehog Crisps', inspired by traditional Romany recipes. The crisps contained no actual hedgehog (thankfully!) and instead were flavoured with pork and herbs to recreate the animal's supposed taste. Still, trading standards weren't amused and insisted Lewis change the name to 'Hedgehog Flavour'.

A MUCH SWEETER SPIN: The hedgehog cake!

Thankfully, these days the only hedgehogs we eat are made of cake. The famous hedgehog cake first appeared in English cookbooks in the eighteenth century as a charming almond-paste dessert shaped like the animal.

I HEART HEDGEHOGS

One early recipe comes from Hannah Glasse's 1747 classic *The Art of Cookery Made Plain and Easy*, which describes forming a hedgehog out of sweet almond paste, covering it with sliced almonds for 'spines', and serving it surrounded by custard or wine cream.

By the 1800s, the recipe for hedgehog cake had evolved. In Addison Ashburn's 1807 cookbook, *The Family Director*, a sponge cake or a French roll became the base, soaked in brandy and wine, and decorated with almond 'spines'. It's easy to see why the idea stuck. Today, the chocolatey, spiky hedgehog cake lives on as a retro British favourite.

AN EIGHTEENTH-CENTURY RECIPE FOR HEDGEHOG CAKE

This recipe for a hedgehog cake was published in English cookbook author Hannah Glasse's *The Art of Cookery Made Plain and Easy* in 1747.

To make a Hedge Hog.

Take two pounds of sweet almonds blanched, beat them well in a mortar, with a little canary and orange-flower water, to keep them from oiling. Make them into a stiff paste, then beat in the yolks of twelve eggs, leave out five of the whites, put to it a pint of cream, sweeten it with sugar, put in a half a pound of sweet butter melted, set it on a furnace or slow fire, and keep continually stirring till it is stiff enough to be made into the form of a hedgehog, then stick it full of blanched almonds slit, and stuck up like the bristles of a hedgehog, then put it into a dish. Take a pint of cream, and the yolks of four eggs beat up, and mix with the cream: sweeten to

I HEART HEDGEHOGS

your palate, and keep them stirring over a slow fire all the time till it is hot, then pour it into your dish round the hedgehog; let it stand till it is cold, and serve it up.

Or you may make a fine hartshorn-jelly, and pour into the dish, which will look very pretty. You may eat wine and sugar with it, or eat it without. Or cold cream sweetened, with a glass of white wine in it, and the juice of a Seville orange, and pour it into the dish. It will be pretty for change. This is a pretty side-dish at a second course, or in the middle for supper, or in a grand desert. Plump two currants for the eyes.

'OFTEN WHEN HE WENT TO THE CITY WITH THE OTHER PEASANTS, THEY WOULD MOCK HIM AND ASK HIM WHY HE HAD NO CHILDREN. HE FINALLY BECAME ANGRY, AND WHEN HE RETURNED HOME, HE SAID, "I WILL HAVE A CHILD, EVEN IF IT IS A HEDGEHOG."'

Jacob and Wilhelm Grimm,
'Hans My Hedgehog'

HOLY HEDGEHOGS

While people in Britain once saw hedgehogs as mischievous and sinister, in many other parts of the world these animals have been revered as sacred and full of wisdom.

In Ancient Egypt, hedgehogs symbolised rebirth. The image of these animals waking from hibernation made them a perfect sign of new life.

In China, the hedgehog is one of five sacred animals – alongside the fox, weasel, snake and rat. In Chinese culture, the hedgehog is respected, and not to be messed with.

In Slavic folklore, the hedgehog is seen as the keeper of knowledge and order, and a symbol of magical power.

And in an old Veps legend (from the Veps people of Finland) a giant hedgehog helped create the world itself! When the Earth was nothing but a great lake, the hedgehog brought up soil and sand on its spines to form dry land.

HOGS IN HISTORY AND FOLKLORE

Hedgehogs even appear in Lithuanian and Latvian creation stories. When God accidentally made the Earth too big for the heavens, a clever hedgehog suggested he squeeze it smaller – creating the mountains in the process. As a reward, God gave the hedgehog its spiky coat of needles.

THE MUSEUM OF ANCIENT HEDGEHOGS

Ancient civilizations have celebrated and represented the hedgehog in art, jewellery and even baby toys. These are some of the most fascinating ancient artefacts featuring these spiny mammals.

Buried with Mummies
In Ancient Egyptian art, hedgehogs were linked to rebirth. Some desert hedgehogs retreat underground during the summer, when they re-emerged, it appeared to the Ancient Egyptians as if they were 'reborn' from the underworld. Because of this, hedgehog figurines were often included in mummy wrappings as a symbol of renewal and protection in the afterlife.

Bling and Rattles
In Ancient Egypt, hedgehogs were also seen as apotropaic creatures, believed to ward off evil. Thought to be animals immune to venom and toxins, Ancient

Egyptians would wear a hedgehog amulet, believing it would transfer this protection to humans. An Ancient Egyptian rattle shaped like a hedgehog to scare off malevolent spirits and dangers was also discovered by archaeologists.

Chinese Clay Vessels
Hedgehogs have also been part of Chinese culture for millennia. A clay hedgehog-shaped vessel from the Neolithic Xiaoheyan culture, dated between 3,000–2,000 BC, was unearthed in Inner Mongolia.

An Ancient Hedgehog on Wheels
A wheeled asphalt limestone hedgehog statuette is part of a group of objects dating to the Middle Elamite Period (1,500–1,200 BC), which was found in 1904 by famed geologist Jacques de Morgan in the ancient city Susa – in what is now Iran. The little statuette of a hedgehog on wheels was discovered alongside other wheeled animals and fragments of board games, and is now owned by the Louvre.

FROM WITCHY TO WONDERFUL: How hedgehogs got their happy ending

For centuries, the humble hedgehog didn't have the best reputation. Blamed for stealing milk and fruit, it was often tangled up with witchcraft and old superstitions. But by the eighteenth and nineteenth centuries, things began to change.

As the scientific study of nature grew, naturalists finally started describing hedgehogs for what they really were – insect-eating, slug-chomping little pest controllers. Farmers began to see them not as nuisances but as tiny, hardworking allies.

And then came the real game changer: the golden age of children's books in the late Victorian and Edwardian periods. Enter Beatrix Potter's *The Tale of Mrs. Tiggy-Winkle* in 1905 – and with it, one of the most beloved hedgehogs in all of literature.

'HER LITTLE BLACK NOSE WENT SNIFFLE, SNIFFLE, SNUFFLE, AND HER EYES WENT TWINKLE, TWINKLE; AND UNDERNEATH HER CAP – WHERE LUCIE HAD YELLOW CURLS – THAT LITTLE PERSON HAD PRICKLES!'

Beatrix Potter,
The Tale of Mrs. Tiggy-Winkle

MRS. TIGGY-WINKLE: The hedgehog who changed everything

Beatrix Potter's *The Tale of Mrs. Tiggy-Winkle* marked a turning point in how people saw hedgehogs. The story follows Lucie, a little girl who loses her handkerchiefs and goes searching for them – only to find they've been washed and pressed by a tiny hedgehog washerwoman called Mrs. Tiggy-Winkle who lives in the hills. Whether Mrs. Tiggy-Winkle is real or a dream is left uncertain at the end of Potter's story, but one thing is clear: readers fell completely in love with her.

Before *The Tale of Mrs. Tiggy-Winkle*, hedgehogs had been seen as grubby, prickly creatures – useful, perhaps, but hardly adorable. Mrs. Tiggy-Winkle changed all that. Potter's detailed illustrations of Mrs. Tiggy-Winkle turned the once-feared hedgehog into a national treasure, transforming superstitious misunderstanding into admiration. Dressed in her cap and apron, she was neat, kind and endlessly industrious – the very picture of domestic charm.

HOGS IN HISTORY AND FOLKLORE

From then on, hedgehogs became symbols of warmth, homeliness and gentle perseverance in Britain – staples of children's stories and adorable illustrations. As natural history writer Hugh Warwick told the BBC: 'Before 1905 [when *The Tale of Mrs. Tiggy-Winkle* was published] pretty well every reference in stories are of hedgehogs either discarded, dismissed. After 1905, everybody loves the hedgehog.'

The hedgehog suddenly became a cosy emblem of English countryside life. By the 1970s and 1980s, Britain's love affair with hedgehogs was in full swing. Hedgehogs starred in public awareness campaigns – from environmental posters promoting wildlife protection to the popular 'Think Hedgehog!' campaign. The 'Think Hedgehog!' adverts, which ran from 1997 to 2010, taught children about the dangers of crossing familiar roads with the help of two cartoon hedgehogs. This legacy helped cement the hedgehog's image as vulnerable and lovable creatures deserving of our care.

I HEART HEDGEHOGS

THE REAL MRS. TIGGY-WINKLE

Beatrix Potter didn't dream Mrs. Tiggy-Winkle up out of nowhere. The iconic character was based on a real hedgehog! Beatrix Potter kept an entire menagerie of pet animals: mice, frogs, rabbits, even a bat and a lizard named Judy. Among them was her pet hedgehog, affectionately called Mrs. Tiggy, who became the model for her famous illustrations in the book.

Beatrix Potter adored observing her animals, often sketching them in detail for her stories. But Mrs. Tiggy, it seems, wasn't always the most cooperative model. As Potter wrote to her editor Norman Warne on 12 November 1904 (according to Linda Lear's biography on her):

'Mrs. Tiggy as a model is comical; so long as she can go to sleep on my knee she is delighted, but if she is propped up on end for half an hour, she first begins to yawn pathetically, and then she does bite!'

Potter's love for animals fuelled her famous children's books. As well as being an author and illustrator, Potter was also a passionate conservationist, leaving over 4,000 acres of land to the National Trust to protect the landscapes she so loved. Thanks to her – and to Mrs. Tiggy – the hedgehog was forever transformed from a creature of superstition into one of Britain's most beloved icons.

HOG TRIVIA: The Tiggywinkles Wildlife Hospital in Haddenham, Buckinghamshire, is a well-known hospital named after the beloved Beatrix Potter character. Founded in 1978, Tiggywinkles Wildlife Hospital treats injured hedgehogs and other species of British wildlife.

It also has a visitor centre which is home to some of the hospital's permanent animals who cannot be returned to the wild, such as blind hedgehogs, for example. The centre also allows visitors to see some of the work Tiggywinkles Hospital does first-hand.

'OBSERVE THE WAY THE HEDGEHOG BUILDS HER NEST, TO FRONT THE NORTH OR SOUTH, OR EAST OR WEST; FOR IF TIS TRUE THAT COMMON PEOPLE SAY, THE WIND WILL BLOW THE QUITE CONTRARY WAY. IF BY SOME SECRET ART THE HEDGEHOGS KNOW SO LONG BEFORE, WHICH WAYS THE WINDS WILL BLOW, SHE HAS AN ART WHICH MANY A PERSON LACKS, THAT THINKS HIMSELF FIT TO MAKE ALMANACS'

Anonymous,
Poor Robin's Almanack

HEDGEHOG HALL OF FAME

Mrs. Tiggy-Winkle might be Britain's best-known hedgehog, but she's far from the only famous fictional prickly star! From the blue hero of a best-selling video game franchise to brave children's book characters, hedgehogs have left their mark across films, tv, books and entertainment.

Here are some of the most beloved fictional hedgehogs of all time.

Sonic the Hedgehog

Zooming onto screens in 1991, Sonic the Hedgehog was created by video game company Sega to compete with Nintendo's mascot Mario. The rest is gaming history.

Sega chose a hedgehog because its spiky shape made perfect sense for a character who could roll into a ball, dash around, and knock things over. Other animals were considered for the character – including a dog, armadillo and porcupine. But Sega eventually decided that the hedgehog was the perfect animal for Sonic (of course!).

Known for his super speed, bright blue colour, and golden ring-collecting ways, Sonic became a pop-culture icon and even inspired a blockbuster film series that's earned over $1 billion worldwide.

Mr. Pricklepants (Toy Story 3)

Mr. Pricklepants, the dramatic little hedgehog from *Toy Story 3*, is a toy thespian dressed in lederhosen who belongs to Andy's sister Bonnie. Voiced by former *James Bond* actor Timothy Dalton, he's known for his love of the stage and his dedication to 'staying in character' – even when Woody interrupts him!

Max the Hedgehog (The Hodgeheg by Dick King-Smith)

Max is the brave hero of Dick King-Smith's 1991 children's book *The Hodgeheg*. This little hedgehog dreams of finding a safe way for his family to cross a busy road to reach a park full of food. Funny, heart-warming, and quietly powerful, the story highlights the dangers wildlife face on our roads through the eyes of a small but determined hedgehog.

Still a favourite story book among children today, *The Hodgeheg* reflects the growing environmental awareness of the late twentieth century – showing hedgehogs as intelligent, brave and endearingly vulnerable, continuing the kind image made famous by Mrs. Tiggy-Winkle.

> 'THIS, THEN, WAS THE MAGIC PLACE! HERE HUMANS COULD CROSS IN PERFECT SAFETY! IF HUMANS CAN, WHY NOT HEDGEHOGS?'
>
> Dick King-Smith,
> *The Hodgeheg*

Mr. and Mrs. Hedgehog (The Animals Of Farthing Wood)

In the 1990s' BBC animated series *The Animals of Farthing Wood*, Mr. and Mrs. Hedgehog won over audiences with their gentle, timid nature. In the TV show, the characters join their woodland friends on a dangerous journey to find a new home after humans destroy their forest.

Tragically, Mr. and Mrs. Hedgehog's story ends when they're run over while crossing a road – a moment that deeply moved viewers and drew attention to the real threats that hedgehogs face in modern Britain.

The Queen of Heart's Hedgehogs (Alice's Adventures In Wonderland)

Lewis Carroll famously included hedgehogs in his 1865 novel *Alice's Adventures in Wonderland*. Carroll gave hedgehogs a memorable role in the Queen of Hearts' croquet game – where they served as stubborn balls! (The Queen of Hearts also used flamingos as mallets and soldiers as hoops!) In Disney's 1951 animated film adaptation *Alice in Wonderland*, the scene was reimagined with two brightly coloured hedgehogs, one pink and one green.

Sebastian the Hedgehog (The Hobbit: An Unexpected Journey)

He may only appear briefly, but Sebastian the Hedgehog still manages to steal hearts in Peter Jackson's movie *The Hobbit: An Unexpected Journey*. When the wizard Radagast the Brown finds Sebastian sick from dark magic, he gently nurses him back to health – a sweet reminder of compassion and the connection between all living things.

Hans My Hedgehog (Brothers Grimm)

In the Brothers Grimm tale *Hans My Hedgehog* (1815), a farmer wishes for a child – 'even if it were a hedgehog' – and gets exactly that. His wife gives birth to a boy who is human from the waist down and a hedgehog from the waist up. They then name him 'Hans My Hedgehog'.

'WE ALL MAKE MISTAKES, AS THE HEDGEHOG SAID AS HE CLIMBED OFF THE SCRUBBING BRUSH'

Anne Sullivan Macy

HEDGEHOGS IN VERSE

With their unique and secretive charm, it's no surprise that hedgehogs have captured the imaginations of poets. Here are some of the greatest poems about these tiny prickly creatures.

HOGS IN HISTORY AND FOLKLORE

'Hedgehog, Hamnavoe' by Jen Hadfield

Jen Hadfield is a British poet who, in 2008, became the youngest female writer to be awarded the T. S. Eliot Prize for her collection *Nigh-No-Place*, which includes the poem 'Hedgehog, Hamnavoe'.

In this poem, Hadfield reflects on a chance encounter with a hedgehog during a late-night walk home. 'Hedgehog, Hamnavoe' looks closely at a hedgehog to explore the natural world and life, without turning the animal into a symbol or myth. Hadfield respects the hedgehog as it is – real and unromanticised – and shows that nature can be fascinating and meaningful on its own.

> 'I AM VERY FOND OF HEDGEHOGS WHICH MAKES ME WANT TO SAY, THAT I AM STRUCK WITH WONDER, HOW THERE'S ANY LEFT TODAY.'
>
> Pam Ayres,
> 'In Defence of Hedgehogs'

'In Defence of Hedgehogs' by Pam Ayres

Pam Ayres is the much-loved British poet known for her witty, down-to-earth poetry and entertaining performances of her verses. Ayres wrote 'In Defence of Hedgehogs' in the early 1970s, after being moved by the sad sight of hedgehogs run over on her drive to work each morning.

Though the poem's tone is light and humorous, Ayres originally wrote it out of genuine sadness and compassion for the animals. At the time, the idea that hedgehogs might one day disappear seemed unimaginable – yet today, with their numbers drastically reduced by habitat loss, pesticides and busy roads, she now views the poem with a poignant awareness.

A passionate advocate for hedgehogs, Ayres said in her 2024 book *Doggedly Onward: A Life in Poems*: 'The fight is on to preserve this, our only spiny mammal, and I hope we win.'

I HEART HEDGEHOGS

'The Mower' by Philip Larkin

Philip Larkin was a British poet known for his reflective poems about everyday life, mortality, and the passage of time. Larkin's short, sombre poem 'The Mower' begins with the discovery of a hedgehog accidentally killed by the speaker's lawnmower. The speaker is shocked and guilt-ridden that his actions caused the animal's death.

In Larkin's poem, the hedgehog's death becomes a powerful reminder of how fragile life is and how easily it can be lost. 'The Mower' shows that every small life matters – including that of a hedgehog.

'The Hedgehog' by Paul Muldoon

Paul Muldoon, the Pulitzer Prize-winning Irish poet, explores the secretive and distrusting nature of hedgehogs in his poem 'The Hedgehog'. Comparing hedgehogs to snails, he imagines a conversation between humans and the animal, inviting readers to consider what a hedgehog might say and how we might earn its trust.

'THE MOWER STALLED, TWICE; KNEELING, I FOUND A HEDGEHOG JAMMED UP AGAINST THE BLADES, KILLED. IT HAD BEEN IN THE LONG GRASS.'

Philip Larkin, 'The Mower'

WHAT IS THE 'HEDGEHOG'S DILEMMA'?

The 'hedgehog's dilemma' is a metaphor, coined by German philosopher Arthur Schopenhauer, to explain the challenges of human intimacy. Schopenhauer imagines hedgehogs huddling together for warmth on a cold night – but their sharp spines make closeness painful, forcing them to keep their distance.

Of course, we have now learned that in reality, hedgehogs are solitary creatures who rely on the comfort of a well-built hibernation nest rather than one another for warmth.

HEDGEHOGS ON THE BIG SCREEN

Curl up (in a ball!) and enjoy these films that no hedgehog fan should miss.

Hedgehog in the Fog (1975)
Hedgehog in the Fog is a Russian-language animated short film about a hedgehog who loses his way in the mist while on the way to see his friend. After the fall of the Soviet Union, *Hedgehog in the Fog* became one of the first Soviet cartoons to be distributed in the West. Since then, the animated film has become critically acclaimed and highly influential for its atmospheric visuals and profound themes. Its enduring popularity even inspired a parody on an episode of *Family Guy* and a *Hedgehog in the Fog* statue, that was unveiled in Kyiv, Ukraine in 2009. The wooden sculpture depicts the titular hedgehog sitting on a stump, holding a small sack.

Sonic the Hedgehog (2020)

No list of hedgehog-inspired films would be complete without the *Sonic the Hedgehog* franchise. The 2020 film set the record for the biggest opening weekend for a video game adaptation in America and Canada. It follows a small-town sheriff who teams up with Sonic, an alien hedgehog with supersonic speed, to outsmart a mad scientist determined to harness his powers for world domination. Jim Carrey stars as Sonic's eccentric archenemy Dr. Robotnik.

> 'BLUE ALIEN HEDGEHOGS ARE PEOPLE TOO.'
>
> Maddie,
> *Sonic the Hedgehog*

Miss Potter (2006)

While not strictly about hedgehogs, this biographical film celebrates the author who helped make these animals beloved around the world with her book *The Tale of Mrs. Tiggy-Winkle*. *Miss Potter* follows Beatrix Potter's journey in 1902 – the year she becomes the best-selling children's writer behind *The Tale of Peter Rabbit*. Renée Zellweger stars as Beatrix Potter, with Ewan McGregor as her publisher and fiancé Norman Warne.

The Hedgehog (Le Hérisson, 2009)

This French drama, inspired by Muriel Barbery's novel *The Elegance of the Hedgehog*, isn't about the animal itself but uses the hedgehog as a metaphor for its protagonist – prickly and reserved on the outside, yet sensitive and refined within. The film explores themes of hidden beauty beneath a guarded exterior.

HEDGEHOG LORE FROM AROUND THE WORLD

Hedgehogs have been at the heart of myths and superstitions around the world, symbolising everything from good luck to weather prophets.

Germany
In German folklore, hedgehogs were seen as good luck. A hedgehog nesting nearby promised prosperity and protection, while harming one could bring misfortune. Hedgehogs also became pop culture stars through 'Mecki' the anthropomorphic hedgehog mascot of Hör Zu magazine. From 1951, Steiff produced Mecki dolls along with his family: Micki, Macki and Mucki.

America
Also originating in German folklore, a hedgehog's shadow on Candlemas Day was said to predict six more weeks of winter. German settlers supposedly brought this tradition to Pennsylvania, but since there were no hedgehogs, they used groundhogs instead – giving rise to the modern Groundhog Day.

England

In rural England, hedgehogs were also seen as weather prophets. Spotting one during the day or in winter was taken as a sign of rain or a harsh season ahead, much like the later Groundhog Day tradition in America. Observing the direction of a hedgehog's nest could even indicate wind direction, as noted in the almanac series *Poor Robin's Almanack* (1733).

North Africa

In North African folklore, hedgehogs are clever, magical animals, often outsmarting foxes or wolves. In Moroccan superstition, they are used in folk medicine and magic, for protection against the evil eye, love potions and curing ailments.

Japan

Hedgehogs aren't native to Japan, but they've become popular pets and cultural icons. Called *harinezumi* meaning 'needle mouse', they're sometimes included in zodiac contexts alongside mice or rats, and admired for their cute (*kawaii*) appearance.

HOGS IN HISTORY AND FOLKLORE

SPIKY ROOMMATES:
The rise of pet hedgehogs

Hedgehogs and humans have crossed paths for thousands of years – but they weren't historically kept as household pets.

There are a few exceptions though. Interestingly, the Ancient Greek philosopher Aristotle once wrote about pet hedgehogs kept in homes in Byzantium – not for fun, but for predicting the weather. (Move over groundhogs!) And of course, Beatrix Potter famously had her own pet hedgehog, Mrs. Tiggy, who inspired the much-loved *The Tale of Mrs. Tiggy-Winkle*. But beyond these rare instances, hedgehogs weren't really domesticated companions until much later.

The modern wave of hedgehog-keeping began in the 1980s, when the African pygmy hedgehog became popular as a pet. These miniature hedgehogs, native to parts of Africa, quickly captured hearts around the world with their tiny paws and twitchy noses.

Today, it's still legal to keep African pygmy hedgehogs as pets in the UK, but animal welfare groups like the RSPCA advise against it. Despite their irresistible charm, hedgehogs are nocturnal, solitary, and have complex needs that make domestic life tricky. In short – they're best admired in the wild, not the living room.

'THE MOST FAMOUS HEDGEHOG IN THE WORLD'

If one hedgehog ever earned true celebrity status, it's Darcy the Flying Hedgehog. This tiny star became an internet sensation thanks to her owner Shota Tsukamoto. Tsukamoto, who is based in Tokyo, Japan, would regularly share whimsical photos of Darcy on Instagram.

From posing next to pineapples and lounging in teacups, Darcy's adventures delighted hundreds of thousands of followers on Instagram. Tsukamoto told TODAY.com his goal was to make Darcy 'the most famous hedgehog in the world', and he absolutely succeeded. Sadly, Darcy passed away in 2014, but the hog's adorable photos continue to charm fans on social media.

BE MORE HEDGEHOG

Hedgehogs might be small and unassuming, but they've got some big life lessons to share. Here's what we can learn from their simple and surprisingly wise way of living.

ME-TIME

Sometimes, the happiest number is one. By now we know that hedgehogs love their solitude and don't need a crowd to feel content. They prove that it's okay to find happiness alone and allow yourself some 'me-time' too.

 TIP: *Treat yourself to a pamper night or settle in with a coffee and a good book. Enjoy your own company for a change.*

STAY CURIOUS

A hedgehog's nose never stops twitching. They wander far and wide every night, exploring wild spaces and whatever may catch their interest. Hedgehogs know that curiosity keeps life fun. Just like hedgehogs, when we follow our curiosity, we discover more about the world – and about ourselves.

 TIP: *Go for a long walk somewhere you've never been – a park, a trail or a green space off your usual route.*

PROTECT YOUR PEACE

When life gets too much, hedgehogs roll up into a ball. You don't need spines, but it's perfectly fine to take a break, rest, and protect your energy when things feel overwhelming.

 TIP: *Say no when you need to. Rest without guilt – your peace is worth it.*

I HEART HEDGEHOGS

APPRECIATE THE QUIET MOMENTS OF THE NIGHT

The world isn't only peaceful at dawn – the night-time has its own kind of wondrous calm. And hedgehogs know this more than anyone else. Hedgehogs thrive in those quiet dark hours, enjoying the stillness while everyone else rests. You can take a cue from them too and let the calm of the evening soothe you too.

TIP: Make yourself a hot chocolate once everyone's gone to bed. Enjoy the peace, the quiet, and the moment just for you.

BE MORE HEDGEHOG

HAVE AN ADVENTUROUS PALATE

Hedgehogs will eat just about anything – they're not fussy, and they're not afraid to try something new. A little openness at mealtimes can make life more interesting. So, why not turn your next meal into an adventure?

 TIP: *Skip your usual takeaway or favourite restaurant. Try a dish you've never had before. Go beyond pizza and explore a cuisine that's bold and different.*

HEDGEHOG HELPERS UNITE

So far in this book, we've explored the fascinating history and habits of hedgehogs – from their beleaguered, witchy past, once hunted as vermin, to their place today as beloved garden visitors. We've followed hedgehogs through the seasons, discovering their quirks and clever survival tricks. Now it's time to learn how we can help them thrive.

I HEART HEDGEHOGS

There was a time in Britain when spotting a hedgehog in your garden was almost guaranteed. You might hear one snuffling in the flowerbeds at night, or find a little ball of spines tucked beneath the shed. But sadly, that's not so common anymore. Hedgehog numbers have fallen sharply across the country, and these once-familiar faces are now officially classed as a vulnerable species in the UK.[1] Since the year 2000, hedgehog numbers have dropped by around half in rural areas and by a third in towns and cities.

So what's gone wrong?

It's a mix of things. As we've built more homes and roads, hedgehogs have lost much of their natural habitat – the wild corners, tangled hedgerows, and log piles they depend on for nesting and hunting. Fences without gaps block their nightly routes, tidy gardens leave nowhere to hide, while pesticides and slug pellets strip away their food supply.

On top of this, hazards like strimmers, netting and steep-sided ponds can cause injury or worse.

---

[1] Listed as vulnerable to extinction on the UK's Red List and the status of the European Hedgehog was updated in Oct 2024 to near threatened on the IUCN Red List.

HEDGEHOG HELPERS UNITE

For city hedgehogs, life can feel like a maze of obstacles all standing between them and survival. Road traffic is now one of the hedgehog's biggest killers – an estimated 335,000 hedgehogs are run over each year on Britain's roads. It's a hard world out there for a small, spiky creature.

But here's the good news: **we can make a difference.** Every garden, no matter how small, can become part of the solution. With a few small changes – a gap in the fence, a wild corner for nesting, and a garden free of chemicals – you can turn your patch of green into a little hedgehog haven.

And hedgehogs aren't just cute visitors; they're helpful ones, too. They'll gobble up slugs, beetles and caterpillars, offering natural pest control and keeping your garden in balance.

From making your own hedgehog café, constructing hedgehog highways, to building a hog its own home in your back garden, this chapter will show you exactly how to welcome these creatures back. With a few simple practical steps, we can all do our bit to help Britain's hedgehogs make a comeback.

SIGNS OF A SECRET NIGHT GUEST:
Is a hedgehog visiting your garden?

LOOK OUT FOR HOG POO

Want to know if a hedgehog is tiptoeing through your garden at night? One of the easiest ways to find out (even if it's not the most glamorous) is to keep an eye out for their poo. Hedgehog droppings are usually black or very dark brown, roughly sausage-shaped, and about 1.5 to 5 centimetres long. They often have a slightly shiny, almost metallic look thanks to the beetle shells and insect bits packed inside.

Unlike fox poo, which can be long, twisted, and stuffed with fur or feathers, or cat droppings, that tend to be lighter and looser, hedgehog poo is distinctive. It is usually left in quiet corners where hedgehogs have been foraging. In rescue hedgehogs fed on pet food, the droppings can be softer and a bit stinky, but in the wild, they're usually firm and full of tiny sparkles.

FOOTPRINTS IN THE NIGHT

Another clue that a hedgehog is wandering in your garden is footprints. Hedgehogs have five toes on each foot. The front feet are wide and hand-like, while the back feet are longer and narrower. Their tracks are usually 2 to 3 centimetres wide, but unless the ground is soft or muddy, you might not see them.

To make spotting them easier, you can create a simple tracker: fill a baking tray with wet sand, put some cat food in the middle, and check the tray in the morning for tiny footprints.

A footprint tunnel – which can be purchased online – is another reliable method. It consists of small plastic triangles with inked inserts that record a hedgehog's visit as it sneaks in for a snack.

I HEART HEDGEHOGS

HOG TRIVIA: Don't be surprised if your garden has more than one secret visitor. Hedgehogs tend to 'do the rounds' at night, visiting several gardens in an area. If you're lucky, you might actually have different individuals sneaking past your plants every night.
So that adorable hedgehog you think is yours is probably just one of several guests.

'FURTHER ON, A HEDGEHOG LAY DEAD ATHWART THE PATH—NAY, MORE THAN DEAD; DECADENT, DISTINCTLY; A SORRY SIGHT FOR ONE THAT HAD KNOWN THE FELLOW IN MORE BUSTLING CIRCUMSTANCES. NATURE MIGHT AT LEAST HAVE PAUSED TO SHED ONE TEAR OVER THIS ROUGH JACKETED LITTLE SON OF HERS, FOR HIS WASTED AIMS, HIS CANCELLED AMBITIONS, HIS WHOLE CAREER OF USEFULNESS CUT SUDDENLY SHORT.'

Kenneth Grahame,
The Golden Age

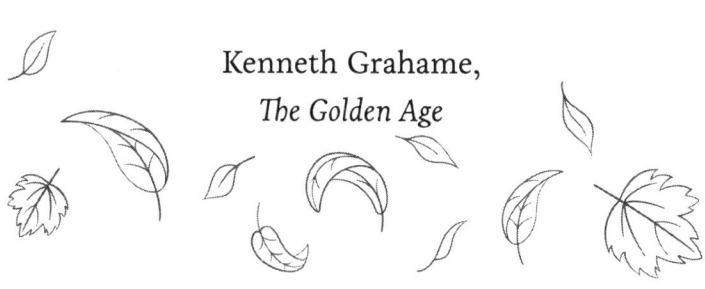

GARDENER'S FRIEND

Easy ways to make your garden hog-friendly and perils to watch out for

Creating a hedgehog-friendly garden is one of the easiest ways to help these wonderful animals. With just a few small tweaks, your outdoor space can become a safe, snack-filled sanctuary for these charming night-time wanderers. Here's how to turn your patch of green into a true hedgehog haven – and a few things to steer clear of along the way.

CREATING A GARDEN FIT FOR A HOG

AVOID BRIGHT NIGHT LIGHTS

Limiting lights in your garden is one of the simplest and most effective ways to support hedgehogs and other nocturnal wildlife. Artificial lighting disrupts their natural behaviour: hedgehogs rely on darkness to forage safely, navigate their territories, and avoid predators. Light pollution can disorient them, reduce feeding opportunities, and fragment the dark corridors they depend on. In many ways, darkness is a habitat in its own right, every bit as vital as access to food, shelter and nesting spaces. By keeping your garden as dark as possible, you help maintain the conditions these night-time creatures have evolved to thrive in.

If you do need lighting, keep it minimal and wildlife-friendly. Use motion sensors so lights turn on only when necessary, and choose fixtures that are shielded and point downwards to prevent glare and sky glow. Warm-toned, low-intensity bulbs are best. This approach not only protects hedgehogs but benefits moths, bats and other nocturnal species whose rhythms depend on natural darkness.

Neighbourhoods can make an even bigger difference by acting together: when whole streets reduce unnecessary lighting, it creates a connected network of safe, dark spaces where nocturnal wildlife can move freely. Small changes in individual gardens can add up to a powerful community effort to preserve the night.

DITCH THE CHEMICALS

Pesticides, herbicides and rodenticides might keep your plants looking neat, but they're bad news for hedgehogs. These chemicals can poison them directly or indirectly by killing off the insects and worms they rely on. Even weed killers make gardens less inviting by stripping away the ground cover hedgehogs love to forage through.

Instead, go natural: try wool pellets, nematode treatments, seaweed, salt, broken eggshells or coffee grounds. Not only will you protect your garden's little ecosystem – you'll also be encouraging hedgehogs to handle pest control for you.

MAKE PONDS SAFE

Ponds are brilliant for wildlife and a vital water source during dry spells. But without an easy exit, they can quickly become death traps for hedgehogs.

To help them out, add a simple escape route to your pond: a gentle slope or ramp made from bricks, logs or sandbags. It should be at least 20 centimetres wide and no steeper than 30 degrees. If you're creating a new pond, build in a shallow 'beach' area so hedgehogs (and other creatures) can climb out safely after a drink or swim.

TANGLED TROUBLE

Loose netting, wire, and even garden games like football or cricket nets can trap hedgehogs, which curl up when frightened rather than fleeing. So, tie nets up when they're not in use, keep fruit and veg netting taut and raised off the ground, and choose thicker mesh or rigid frames when possible. And don't forget the simple stuff – pick up stray litter or bits of wire that could catch a curious hog.

CHECK BEFORE YOU BURN

Bonfires are like five-star hotels to a tired hedgehog looking for a nap – warm, dry and cosy. Unfortunately, that also makes them dangerous. Always move your bonfire pile on the day you plan to light it, so you know there are no hidden guests inside. If that's not possible, surround it with a barrier of steep plastic sheeting to keep hedgehogs out. When lighting a bonfire, start from one side to give any hidden hedgehogs a chance to escape.

MIND THE MACHINERY

Hedgehogs love curling up in long grass and leaf piles – exactly where strimmers and mowers can reach. Always check before cutting and never run robotic lawnmowers at night when hedgehogs are most active. Those silent blades can cause serious injuries to them or worse.

KEEP PETS AND PREDATORS IN CHECK

Badgers are natural predators, but foxes and dogs can also pose a risk. To keep your garden safe, try keeping dogs on leads during dusk and after dark. Dense vegetation, brambles, or purpose-built hog houses (we'll show you how to make your own on page 153) make brilliant safe zones. Hedgehogs will happily tuck themselves away in thick cover where curious noses can't reach.

HOG TRIVIA: Hedgehogs are frequently thought to be covered in fleas, but the ones they carry are usually hedgehog fleas (*Archaeopsylla erinacei*), a species that only survives on hedgehogs. They can't live on humans or pets, so there's no need for concern if one visits your garden.

THE DON'TS FOR HEDGEHOGS

- Don't use slug pellets, rodenticides or harsh garden chemicals – they can poison hedgehogs and their prey.

- Don't leave ponds without an escape route – hedgehogs can drown if they can't get out.

- Don't leave loose netting, wires or litter lying around.

- Don't light bonfires without checking for wildlife first.

- Don't run strimmers or robotic mowers at night.

NEXT-LEVEL HEDGEHOG GARDENING

So, you've already made your garden hedgehog-friendly, why stop there? With a few extra touches, you can turn it into a veritable hog heaven – a wild, welcoming space full of cosy corners and yummy bugs for your spiky neighbours.

PILE IT HIGH

A log pile is the ultimate hedgehog hangout. It offers food, shelter and nesting space all in one. Gather fallen branches, sticks or logs and stack them in a quiet corner. Mix chunky logs with smaller twigs to create secret hidey holes. The older the pile, the better – as it breaks down, it'll attract beetles, grubs and worms (hedgehog favourites!). Top it up occasionally to keep it fresh.

CREATE A COMPOST CORNER

An open compost heap is a magnet for hedgehogs – warm, safe and full of tasty insects. Just remember to check for any sleepy hedgehogs before turning it over. You can still keep a closed compost bin for kitchen scraps, but leave one open heap just for garden waste and wildlife. It's the perfect all-inclusive resort for your resident hogs.

LEAF IT BE

Put down the rake – at least a little! Fallen leaves are nature's best bedding and free insulation for hedgehogs. Let some leaves gather beneath shrubs and hedges to form natural leaf mould, which feeds your soil and encourages the beetles and worms that hedgehogs love. Or you could go one step further and rake leaves into a pile under a hedge – ideal for hedgehogs seeking a nest. But always check before tidying up leaves in autumn or winter to make sure you don't disturb a sleeping prickly guest.

GO WILD IN A CORNER

Every garden needs a touch of wilderness. Let one patch grow untamed with a few tall grasses and brambles. This wild corner will soon become its own little mini nature reserve – offering insects a home and hedgehogs a reliable food source and possibly even shelter at times. Leave it untrimmed all year or give it a gentle tidy every couple of months to keep the natural look going strong.

GROW A WILDFLOWER PATCH

Wildflowers aren't just pretty to look at – they're a buffet and shelter zone for all the insects that hedgehogs love to gobble up. Even a small patch of wild blooms in your garden can make a big difference.

THINK BEYOND THE FENCE

One garden alone can't meet a hedgehog's needs – but together, a neighbourhood of gardens can. Work with your neighbours to create 'hedgehog highways'. These 13 centimetre openings can transform a patchwork of private gardens into a thriving hedgehog network, helping them roam freely and safely in search of food, mates and new adventures. On the next page, you'll learn exactly how to make your own hedgehog highway.

HEDGEHOG HIGHWAYS AND BYWAYS

How to connect gardens for happy wanderers

Hedgehogs travel a long way every night in search of food, mates and a cosy nesting spot for such small creatures. But as our gardens have become tidier and our fences sturdier, these little wanderers are finding their natural routes blocked. Hedgehogs may look independent, but they need our help to get from one garden to another safely. That's where the hedgehog highway comes in.

A hedgehog highway is a simple, ground-level hole or gap in outdoor fences or walls that lets hedgehogs move freely between gardens. Think of it as a mini motorway for wildlife – a safe, quick shortcut between your garden and your neighbour's. With every household that joins in, we create a connected network of gardens, allowing hedgehogs to explore, feed and find shelter without the danger of being stranded.

Making a hedgehog highway is much easier than building a human one – no hard hats or roadworks required! It's also one of the most rewarding ways to make your outdoor space more hedgehog-friendly.

HOW TO MAKE A HEDGEHOG HIGHWAY

YOU'LL NEED
- An outdoor fence panel (or wall/gate)
- A ruler
- A pencil
- A coping saw or small hand saw
- Sandpaper
- And, most importantly, your neighbour's cooperation.

INSTRUCTIONS

Step One: Choose your spot

Pick a sheltered corner of your garden, away from busy roads and paved areas. The goal is to create a safe, quiet passage where hedgehogs can move unseen. If you already have gaps under gates or between fence boards, you can simply widen them.

Step Two: Measure and mark

Using your ruler and pencil, mark a square 13 centimetres x 13 centimetres at the bottom of your fence. This is the perfect size: big enough for hedgehogs, but too small for most pets.

Step Three: Cut your hole
Use your coping saw or small hand saw to carefully cut along your markings. If you're working in wood, drill a small starter hole first to make sawing easier. Once you've finished, sand down any rough edges so there's nothing sharp for hedgehogs to catch on.

Step Four: Replace or reinforce
If you've removed a fence panel to cut your hole, pop it back into place. If your boundary is concrete, you can dig a small tunnel beneath it or use bricks, pipes or cinder blocks to form a passageway. Cinder blocks make excellent tunnels and can help prevent dogs or other pets from using the hole.

Step Five: Test it and tidy up
Make sure your new hole is clear of debris and leads somewhere safe and sheltered. Then stand back and admire your handiwork – you've just built a hog superhighway!

'THE THING ABOUT HEDGEHOGS IS THAT THEY TRAVEL ABSOLUTELY MILES. LOVELY AS IT IS TO HAVE THEM IN THE GARDEN, IF THEY'VE GOT NO CORRIDOR TO TRAVEL ALONG, THEN THEY'RE NOT GOING TO FIND ENOUGH FOOD TO EAT.'

David Attenborough

EXTRA TIPS FOR A BRILLIANT HEDGEHOG HIGHWAY

WORK TOGETHER

Talk to your neighbours. A single garden hole is a great start, but a whole row of connected gardens is even better. Hedgehogs need to roam far and wide through several gardens each night to find enough food. By linking your gardens together, you create a continuous network of safe spaces where they can feed, shelter and move freely. The longer the chain, the better the results – for hedgehogs, and for your local ecosystem too.

ADD A HEDGEHOG HIGHWAY SIGN

You can buy hedgehog highway signs from the People's Trust for Endangered Species (PTES) or the British Hedgehog Preservation Society (BHPS). These are a lovely way to mark the purpose of your new wildlife entrance and encourage others to join in.

PLANT FOR COVER

Hedgehogs prefer to travel under cover, so let grass, ivy or herbaceous plants grow a little longer around your highway entrance. It will make them feel safer from predators and give them somewhere to forage for beetles and worms along the way.

AVOID ROAD EXITS

Never make a hole that leads directly onto a road or driveway. Keep your highways connecting green spaces only, to make sure hedgehogs stay safe as they travel.

GET CREATIVE WITH MATERIALS

If you don't want to cut your fence, remove a brick from the bottom of a wall, or dig a small channel underneath a boundary. Spare piping or old bricks can be used to make neat little tunnels.

COORDINATE WITH CONTRACTORS

Keep an eye out for neighbours doing garden work or replacing fences. It's the perfect opportunity to ask whether they would be keen to have a hedgehog highway added in. Many suppliers now even offer ready-made hedgehog-friendly gravel boards designed with access holes built in.

THINK BEYOND FENCES
If you're feeling extra ambitious, swap solid fences for living hedges. These provide natural shelter, food and extra pathways for hedgehogs.

> HOG TRIVIA: In 2022, Dale Road in the village of Keyworth, Nottinghamshire was named 'Britain's Biggest Hedgehog Street'. The residents had created more than 40 hedgehog highways along that single street. Meanwhile, the village of Kirtlington in Oxfordshire is home to the UK's longest volunteer-run hedgehog highway through 60 properties in the village, some of which have been around since the eighteenth century.

GET YOUR PAWS DIRTY

Give a hog a home

Every garden deserves a little wild magic – and few guests are as charming as the humble hedgehog. With a little effort, you can offer the perfect refuge for a hedgehog right in your own back garden – by making a hog house.

A hog house is a cosy, sheltered hideaway that gives hedgehogs a safe place to rest during the day and hibernate through the winter. In the wild, they'd make their nests in log piles, brambles or deep leaf litter. But our neat modern gardens don't always offer hedgehogs the safe spaces they need to rest and hide. Building or buying a hog house is one of the simplest ways to make your garden more welcoming. A well-made one provides the perfect substitute for natural shelters, keeping hedgehogs safe from predators, bad weather and everyday garden hazards.

As mentioned earlier, you can of course leave a patch of your garden to grow wild, build a log pile or set up a compost heap – hedgehogs love those for shelter too. But if you want to go one step further, creating a dedicated hog house is a fun project that really makes a difference. Tuck it into a quiet, shaded corner of your garden, and you might just find a hedgehog moving in before you know it.

'WHEN THEY HIDE THEMSELVES IN THEIR DEN, THEY HAVE A NATURALL UNDERSTANDING OF THE TURNING OF THE WIND, SOUTH AND NORTH […] THE WILD ONES HAVE TWO HOLES IN THEIR CAVE, THE ONE NORTH, THE OTHER SOUTH, OBSERVING TO STOP THE MOUTH AGAINST THE WIND, AS THE SKILFUL MARINER TO STERE & TURNE THE RUDDER OR SAILS.'

Edward Topsell,
Historie of Four-Footed Beasts

HOW TO MAKE A HOG HOUSE

There are two main ways to build a hog house – one way is quick and easy while the second way is a little more advanced but perfect for the enthusiastic DIY-er. However, both hog houses will provide a welcoming bolthole for these precious prickly darlings.

THE EASY DIY HOG HOUSE
You don't need to be a master builder for this option – just a few straightforward materials will do. This easy hog house will take around 1 hour to make.

YOU'LL NEED
- A plastic storage box, planter or milk crate (make sure it has air holes)
- A saw or sharp knife (for cutting the entrance)
- Dry leaves or pet-safe straw for bedding
- Soil, turf or leaves to cover the top for camouflage

I HEART HEDGEHOGS

INSTRUCTIONS

Step One: Flip the box upside down so the open side faces downwards.

Step Two: Cut an entrance at one end – 13 centimetres x 13 centimetres is perfect.

Step Three: Line the inside with a soft bedding layer of dry leaves or straw, rather than synthetic man-made bedding or anything that retains moisture.

Step Four: Cover the top of the box and its sides with soil, turf or leaves to blend it into the surroundings and keep it insulated.

Step Five: Place it in a shady, quiet corner of your garden, ideally against a fence or hedge. And that's it – a no-fuss way to give hedgehogs a safe space to rest!

THE TRICKY DIY HOG HOUSE

If you'd like something more durable and a good weekend project, try building a wooden hog house. Hedgehogs seem to love homemade houses made from untreated wood, ideally UK-grown softwoods like larch, Douglas fir or red cedar. These timbers are naturally weather-resistant and much safer for wildlife than pre-treated wood, which can contain harmful chemicals.

YOU'LL NEED

- Untreated wood cut to these measurements:
  Sides: 30 cm high x 30 cm wide
  Top: 30 cm x 40 cm
  Base: 30 cm x 40 cm
  Front and back: 30 cm x 40 cm
- Tunnel: 13 cm high x 30 cm long
- Batons (to secure the lid and slightly raise the box off the ground)
- Dry leaves or pet-safe straw for bedding
- Soil, turf or leaves to cover the top for camouflage.

I HEART HEDGEHOGS

INSTRUCTIONS
Step One: Build the main box
Take the sides, front, back and base panels and attach them together to form a simple rectangular box with one open side for the entrance. Make sure the edges are flush so the house is sturdy. Then attach the tunnel to the open entrance – this long, narrow passage helps keep hedgehogs safe from predators and curious pets.

Step Two: Make the roof removable
Instead of nailing it down permanently, leave it loose or attach it with simple hinges or clips. This way, you can easily lift the roof once a year to clean out old bedding and keep the house fresh and safe.

Step Three: Protect against damp
Drill a few small drainage holes in the base to let water escape. Then use small batons to lift the house slightly off the ground – this keeps the floor dry and the hedgehogs comfortable.

Step Four: Add bedding
Fill the house with dry leaves or straw (not synthetic man-made bedding) to create a warm, insulated space for hedgehogs to rest and sleep.

Step Five: Camouflage and weatherproof
Cover the top of the hog house with soil, turf, or more leaves. This hides the house from predators and adds extra protection against rain and wind.

Step Six: Position your hog house
Place it along a garden boundary, under a hedge, or in a quiet, shaded area, ideally within about 5 metres of your home. Hedgehogs prefer sheltered spots, so choose a location that feels safe and secluded.

I HEART HEDGEHOGS

HOG TRIVIA: As there are no native hedgehogs in North America, these prickly creatures sometimes get lost in translation on American TV shows. In a few US versions of British programmes (like *Bob the Builder* and *Littlest Pet Shop*), hedgehogs have even been replaced or mistaken for porcupines instead to avoid confusion for American viewers.

EXTRA TIPS FOR YOUR HOG HOUSE

HIDEAWAY HEAVEN

Choose a quiet, shaded area away from busy paths and direct sunlight. Hedgehogs like privacy.

TRICKY ENTRANCE, SAFE HEDGEHOG

Hedgehogs need a safe space where predators can't reach them, so make the entrance tricky. You can add a short tunnel at the front of the hog house – about 30 centimetres long is enough – which hedgehogs can easily crawl through but keeps foxes and badgers out. If your design doesn't have a tunnel, place a small internal barrier or dividing wall between the entrance and the main nesting area. This creates a safe buffer zone where your hedgehog can rest or hibernate in peace.

KEEP THE KITCHEN OUTSIDE

Food and water should be placed nearby, not inside. The smell of food can attract unwanted visitors or disturb hibernating hedgehogs.

SPRING CLEAN
Clean your hog house in March or April, after hibernation but before the breeding season begins. If a hedgehog is still inside, wait until it leaves naturally and never disturb a nesting mother.

THE TWIG TEST
Place a small twig over the entrance. If it's moved when you check it the following day, you'll know someone's checked in.

GET CURIOUS WITH A CAMERA
You could even consider setting up a small wildlife trail camera near the entrance of your hog house to see who is visiting after dark. You might be surprised by how many garden guests you have.

IF YOU'RE FEELING LAZY
If you would rather not build your own hog house, you can buy ready-made hedgehog homes online.

'THE HEDGEHOG THAT IS LOADEN WITH APPLES SHALL REBUILD HER, AND UNTO THE SMELL OF THE APPLES THE FOWLS OF MANY FORESTS SHALL FLY TOGETHER.'

Geoffrey of Monmouth

THE HEDGEHOG CAFE:
What to feed (and what not to)

Ever thought about opening up a café for the cutest night-time diners? Well now you can do just that for hedgehogs!

Leaving food and water out in your garden can help these animals survive and thrive. During hot, dry spells or the colder months, insects can be hard to come by, so a reliable snack can make all the difference.

By providing a safe spot to eat in peace, you're giving local hedgehogs a helping hand – and a little restaurant they're sure to love.

WHAT'S ON THE HEDGEHOG MENU

Hedgehogs can enjoy a little extra food throughout most of the year. In spring, it helps them shake off hibernation, while in summer and autumn a few tasty treats can support young hoglets as they grow, and help adults build the fat they need for the winter months.

The best menu options include meat-based wet cat or dog food, especially chicken or beef flavours (no fish please). Crunchy dry cat biscuits are also good options and last longer than wet food. You can also buy specialist hedgehog food from garden centres or online (just check the ingredients, as quality can vary). Offer fresh, clean water in a shallow dish tucked in a shaded spot – perfect for hot or dry weather when natural water sources disappear.

 TOP TIP: *When choosing any of these foods, make sure meat is the first ingredient on the label.*

WHAT NOT TO SERVE YOUR SPIKY GUESTS

Some foods that seem harmless can actually be dangerous for hedgehogs. Bread and milk are an absolute no-go. Milk particularly can cause diarrhoea and dehydration in hedgehogs. Mealworms, sunflower seeds and peanuts are also not a good choice for hogs – and live mealworms should not be allowed to escape into the wild. They are high in phosphorus but low in calcium, which can lead to brittle bones or Metabolic Bone Disease (MBD). Honey, sugar, fruit and cereal aren't suitable for these animals either, as hedgehogs can't digest them properly and they can cause tooth decay.

 TOP TIP: *If you feed garden birds, it's a good idea to place trays under feeders so seeds and nuts don't fall to the ground where hungry hedgehogs might find them overnight.*

SERVING UP A SAFE SUPPER

The best time to serve your hedgehog dinner is at dusk, when they're most active. Keep the food fresh by removing uneaten portions in the morning and replacing them with new offerings each evening. Moving the food around the garden from time to time also encourages natural foraging and helps prevent competition between hedgehogs. Heavy ceramic bowls work well because they're hard to tip over and washing them regularly (separately from your own dishes) keeps bacteria at bay.

HOW TO MAKE A HEDGEHOG FEEDING STATION

Fancy taking your hog hospitality up a notch? A homemade hedgehog feeding station – or 'hog café' – is the perfect way to serve supper in style. It keeps food dry, safe from greedy guests like cats and foxes, and reserves a spot just for your prickly visitors. You can buy a ready-made hedgehog feeding station, but it's easy (and much more fun) to build your own.

YOU'LL NEED

- A plastic storage box or wooden crate with a lid (ideally around 30 cm wide x 40 cm long x 30 cm high, but bigger is fine)
- A ruler and pencil to mark out measurements
- Strong scissors, a Stanley knife or a jigsaw for cutting the entrance
- Strong tape (like duct tape) or sandpaper to smooth any rough edges
- Newspaper or old cardboard to line the base
- Two small, heavy ceramic bowls – one for food, one for water
- A brick or heavy stone to weigh down the lid

INSTRUCTIONS
Step One: Create the entrance
Measure and cut a square entrance hole around 13 centimetres x 13 centimetres on one of the short sides of your box. This size is large enough for a hedgehog but too small for cats, foxes and most other garden visitors.

Step Two: Smooth it out
Tape or sand down any sharp edges from the cutting to prevent injury. If you're using plastic, a layer of duct tape around the edges works perfectly.

Step Three: Prepare the inside
Line the base of the box with newspaper or cardboard – it'll absorb moisture and make cleaning easier. Place your bowls at the furthest end from the entrance to keep food and water out of reach of rain or other paws besides hedgehogs.

Step Four: Secure the lid

If your box has a lid, fix it on and place a brick or heavy stone on top to stop foxes or cats from nudging it open. If you're using the box upside-down, put the lid on the ground to act as a base instead.

Step Five: Position it well

Choose a quiet, shaded spot in your garden – ideally along a fence line, hedge or under shrubs. Hedgehogs like sheltered, tucked-away corners.

KEEPING YOUR HOG CAFÉ CLEAN

Even the best cafés need a good tidy-up. Because hedgehogs often share feeding stations, keeping things clean helps everyone stay healthy. Swap out the newspaper lining each day, and wash the food and water bowls regularly using a separate sponge and bucket – keep them out of your kitchen sink to avoid spreading germs! Every couple of weeks, move the café to a new spot in the garden to stop any pesky parasites from settling in.

And how do you know if you've had visitors? Look out for telltale signs like crumbs, droppings or tiny muddy footprints – the surest proof your café has been a hit!

SPOTTED A HEDGEHOG? HERE'S WHAT TO DO

Hedgehogs are mostly nocturnal, so seeing one in daylight isn't always normal – but it's not always an emergency either. Sometimes a hedgehog might be out during the day for natural reasons: a pregnant or nursing female collecting food, a hedgehog moving home after its nest was disturbed, or simply foraging during short summer nights. If the hedgehog is moving purposefully and seems alert, it usually doesn't need help and you should leave it well alone.

However, there are some warning signs for when a hedgehog does need assistance. If you notice any of the following symptoms or signs, it's time to step in:

- Lethargic or motionless – hedgehogs don't sunbathe. If it's lying still in the open, something may be wrong.

- Flies swarming often indicates injury or illness.

- Wobbly walking or struggling to move.

- Visible injuries such as cuts or wounds.

- Trapped in netting, garden drains or ponds.

- Hoglets alone – baby hedgehogs out in the day without an adult is often a sign they need help.

HOW TO SAFELY HANDLE AN ADULT HEDGEHOG

- Protect your hands: Handle the hedgehog with thick gardening gloves or a folded towel.

- Be gentle and calm: Hedgehogs are easily startled.

- Lift carefully: If curled, scoop it up as a ball; if uncurled, slide a hand under its tummy.

- Provide a safe home: Place it in a deep cardboard or plastic box lined with a towel or fleece. Make sure the container is escape-proof as hedgehogs are good climbers.

SPOTTED A HEDGEHOG? HERE'S WHAT TO DO

- Keep it warm: If it's very cold weather, you could add a wrapped hot water bottle. Checking that the hot water bottle is comfortably warm (not boiling) and make sure the hedgehog has space to move away from the heat if needed.

- Quiet space: Keep the box somewhere calm, dark and away from children or pets.

- Food and water: Offer a small portion of meaty cat or dog food and fresh water, but don't force it to eat or drink.

- Seek advice promptly: Contact a local hedgehog rescue or wildlife rehabilitator for guidance.

I HEART HEDGEHOGS

HANDLING HOGLETS

- Baby hedgehogs need extra care – handling them incorrectly can be dangerous for them.

- Always use thick gloves when handling hoglets: Your scent can scare the mother.

- Move the nest carefully: If intact, transfer it to a secure box lined with a towel or fleece. If the mother is present, place her separately.

- Keep the hoglets warm: Maintain warmth with a wrapped hot water bottle if needed, checking that the hot water bottle is comfortably warm (not boiling) and letting the babies move away if they get too hot. Check the temperature regularly.

- When to intervene: If the mother is present and the babies are unharmed, leave them alone and monitor. However, if you find the hoglets abandoned and the mother doesn't return after several hours, contact a vet or hedgehog rescue immediately. Raising baby hedgehogs at home isn't recommended – they need specialist care, diet and housing to survive.

Note: If you accidentally disturb a nest but both mother and babies are safe, simply cover it back up and leave them be.

> # 'THORNY HEDGEHOGS, BE NOT SEEN'
>
> William Shakespeare,
> *A Midsummer Night's Dream*

I HEART HEDGEHOGS

SAY CHEESE (QUIETLY):
How To Photograph Hedgehogs

SPOTTED A HEDGEHOG? HERE'S WHAT TO DO

Spotted a hedgehog padding through your garden and fancy a photo? Go for it – just remember, their comfort always comes first. These shy, night-time explorers prefer to keep things low-key, so the trick is to watch quietly and let them do their thing.

To get the best shots without bothering your spiky stars, keep a little distance and never try to touch or move them. Make sure to skip the flash – it's dazzling for hedgehogs. If you're after that perfect shot, it might also be easier to record a short video of the hog and pick your favourite still frame from the footage later.

Even better, you could set up a wildlife or night-vision camera in your garden – there are many on the market now that are relatively inexpensive. That way, you'll see all their midnight wanderings without having to sneak around in the dark yourself.

Above all, stay calm, quiet and patient. The best hedgehog photos are the ones where they don't even notice you're there.

HEDGEHOG HEROES

Ready to join the hedgehog hero squad? You're not alone! To help inspire you, here is a list of some of the fantastic charities, organisations and initiatives all set up to protect our prickly little friends and help them thrive in our gardens, parks and beyond.

Whether you want to learn how to care for a hedgehog in need, create safe spaces in your neighbourhood, or simply spread the word, these heroes have got your back.

BRITISH HEDGEHOG PRESERVATION SOCIETY (BHPS)

The ultimate hedgehog heroes of the UK. This charity is all about protecting our prickly pals through education, campaigning and funding important research. They're the go-to folks if you find a sick or injured hedgehog, and they keep a handy list of rescue centres ready to help.

PEOPLE'S TRUST FOR ENDANGERED SPECIES (PTES)

Nature's defenders with a soft spot for hedgehogs. PTES works hard to save endangered animals and their homes, with hedgehogs high on their priority list. They run surveys, provide support and team up with BHPS to give hedgehogs a fighting chance.

HEDGEHOG STREET

The coolest neighbourhood-watch for hedgehogs. Launched in 2011 by BHPS and PTES, this campaign invites you to become a 'Hedgehog Champion' by making your garden a hedgehog highway hotspot.

THE WILDLIFE TRUSTS

A bunch of local wildlife lovers across the UK who work tirelessly to protect all things wild and wonderful. They run fun campaigns like 'Be More Hedgehog' and share top tips on turning your garden into a hedgehog heaven.

TIGGYWINKLES WILDLIFE HOSPITAL

The hedgehog's five-star recovery centre in Buckinghamshire. Open 24/7, this hospital cares for poorly, injured and orphaned hedgehogs (and other British wildlife), giving them the TLC they need to get back on their feet.

HEDGEHOG FRIENDLY CAMPUS

Calling all universities and institutions! This project encourages you to turn your grounds into hedgehog-friendly hangouts, helping these spiky little explorers thrive while you study or work.

TEST YOUR HOG KNOWLEDGE
(true or false)

1. The hedgehog's closest relative is a shrew.

2. Hedgehogs have one lifelong mate.

3. Hedgehogs have been known to survive snake bites.

4. Hedgehogs' spines appear an hour after they are born.

5. Hedgehogs can shoot their spines like porcupines.

6. Hedgehogs should be fed milk.

7. Hedgehogs breathe only once every few minutes during hibernation.

8. Hedgehogs are strong swimmers and climbers.

9. Humans have more teeth than hedgehogs.

10. Baby hedgehogs are called hoglets.

1. TRUE; 2. FALSE; 3. TRUE; 4. TRUE; 5. FALSE; 6. FALSE; 7. TRUE; 8. TRUE; 9. FALSE; 10. TRUE

YOUR HOG-FRIENDLY GARDEN CHECKLIST

Feeling overwhelmed by everything you've just taken in? You're not alone. This simple checklist breaks what can feel like a big responsibility into manageable, tick-off-as-you-go steps. There's no need to do it all at once – every small action helps make outdoor spaces safer for these nighttime wanderers.

EASY:
First steps for a hog-friendly garden

- ☐ Check for signs of hedgehog visitors (poo, footprints or camera footage).

- ☐ Minimize unnecessary light pollution.

- ☐ Ditch pesticides, slug pellets and rodenticides – go chemical-free.

- ☐ Keep your garden litter-free (no wires, netting or rubbish lying around).

- ☐ Tie up or raise loose garden netting to prevent entanglement.

- ☐ Always check grass, leaf piles and compost piles before mowing or strimming.

YOUR HOG-FRIENDLY GARDEN CHECKLIST

☐ Never run robotic lawnmowers at night.

☐ Move bonfire piles on the day you burn them (because hedgehogs love to nest inside).

☐ Keep a shallow dish of fresh water in the garden, especially in dry weather.

☐ Provide meat-based wet cat or dog food or dry cat biscuits at dusk.

INTERMEDIATE: Create a safe spiky haven

- ☐ Make your pond hedgehog-safe with a ramp, gentle slope or 'beach' exit.

- ☐ Make a hedgehog highway in your garden.

- ☐ Leave areas of long grass or wild plants for cover and foraging.

- ☐ Create a leaf pile under hedges for natural bedding and to attract insects.

- ☐ Start an open compost heap (check for sleepy hogs before turning it).

- ☐ Build a log pile with mixed sticks and logs for shelter and to attract bugs.

YOUR HOG-FRIENDLY GARDEN CHECKLIST

☐ Buy or build an easy DIY hog house (see page 153).

☐ Put out food and water near the hog house, but never inside it.

☐ Do the twig test – place a twig at the entrance to see if it's been used.

ADVANCED:
Make a prickly paradise

- ☐ Build a wooden hog house (advanced DIY version, see page 155).

- ☐ Add a short tunnel or internal wall to the hog house entrance for predator protection.

- ☐ Set up a hedgehog feeding station or hog café.

- ☐ Grow a wildflower patch to attract insects for hedgehogs.

- ☐ Coordinate with neighbours to create other hedgehog highways (13 cm x 13 cm holes).

- ☐ Mark your hedgehog highway with a PTES or BHPS sign to inspire others.

- ☐ Replace solid fences with living hedges for natural corridors.

YOUR HOG-FRIENDLY GARDEN CHECKLIST

☐ Use a trail camera to track your garden's nightly visitors.

BONUS: Seasonal Reminders

Spring
Clean hog houses, top up log piles and start feeding if food is scarce.

Summer
Keep water topped up; retain wild areas.

Autumn
Check leaf piles carefully before raking and provide extra food to help fatten hogs for hibernation.

Winter
Don't disturb sleeping hogs.

We all heart hedgehogs!

Thank you for reading this book and for choosing to help our prickly friends. I hope these pages have deepened your understanding of their secretive lives and sparked a renewed desire to protect them for years to come.